BAGUA &

an intersection of the straight and curved

八卦掌形意拳

An Anthology of Articles from the *Journal of Asian Martial Arts*
Compiled by Michael A. DeMarco, M.A.

All articles in this anthology were originally published in the *Journal of Asian Martial Arts*.
Listed according to the table of contents for this anthology:

Brinkman, M. & Stubenbaum, D, (1994), Vol. 3 No. 4, pp. 52-63
Phelps, S. (1998), Vol. 7, No. 4, pp. 60-81
Pittman, A. (1999), Vol. 8, No. 1, pp. 56-73
Craig, K. (1999), Vol. 8 No. 2, pp. 62-79
Lin, R. Lin-yi (2001), Vol. 10 No. 3, pp. 64-75
Lin, R. Lin-yi (2002), Vol. 11 No. 3, pp. 66-83
Henning, S. (2005), Vol. 14 No. 3, pp. 22-29
Smith, J. & Bild, M. (2005), Vol. 14, No. 3, pp. 38-53
Henning, S. (2006), Vol. 15 No. 3, pp. 54-65
Cartmell, T. (2004), Vol. 18, No. 4, pp. 46-63
Joern, T. (2010), Vol. 19, No. 4, pp. 84-107
Hong, Dzehan, P. (2012), In *Asian Martial Arts:*
Constructive Thoughts & Practical Applications, pp. 74-77

Book and cover design by Via Media Publishing Company
Edited by Michael A. DeMarco, M.A.

Cover illustration

Hong Dzehan (洪澤漢), a stellar master of bagua and xingyi, teaches in Taipei, Taiwan.
He can be found on Facebook by searching his name using Chinese characters.
Photography by Christopher Bates.

ISBN: 9781893765337

w w w . v i a m e d i a p u b l i s h i n g . c o m

contents

preface

Baguaquan and xingyiquan are two styles that complement each other as yin does yang. Bagua is known for its circular movements and its practice of "circle walking." Xingyi embodies characteristic linear movements said to be derived from the logical strategies for using spear and staff.

How fortunate we are to include writings in this anthology by leading authorities on these styles. Separated into three sections, the first features bagua. Allen Pittman presents five variations of the "single palm change", followed by an overview of the Yin Fu bagua linage and an interview with He Jinbao focusing on training, fighting skills, teaching and learning. Travis Joern examines how a martial artist can apply the theoretical aspects of the *Book of Changes* to bagua training. Hong Dzehan—son of Hong Yixiang, stellar master of the three internal systems—then shares some of his personal experiences and favorite bagua techniques.

Section two contains chapters on xingyi. The interview with Luo Dexiu questions the proper way to study xingyi from the beginning to the advanced levels. Robert Yu compares American boxing with xingyi's pragmatic fighting techniques and in the following chapter he recounts in detail how it was to study under Hong Yixiang in Taiwan nearly forty years ago. Stanley Henning gives a travelogue of a trip to Shanxi Province—the home of xingyiquan—and then discusses Che Style xingyi training methods as taught by Dr. Wu Chaoxiang, including the five element theory, twelve animal forms, two-person routines, and spear training.

The third section presents some commonalities in what many refer to as the "internal arts": bagua, xingyi, and taiji. The chapter on Fu family style beautifully details how they incorporated the essential elements of taiji, xingyi, and bagua into their majestic *sixiangquan* (four image boxing). Marcus Brinkman relates many of the unique insights and experiences he had during his extensive study with Lo Dexiu and Hong Yixiang, including internal development and fighting applications. Tim Cartmell provides the final chapter which explains the key concepts of "sticking and following" as they apply to the throwing methods of the Chinese internal martial arts.

The rich content in this anthology comes from the rare academic and hands-on experience of those presented in chapters here. Readers will no doubt benefit from the practical practice tips as well as the other cultural details these wonderful authors share.

Michael A. DeMarco, Publisher
Santa Fe, New Mexico, August 2016

chapter 1

Single Palm Change
Bagua's Core Movement

by Allen Pittman

All form photographs courtesy of Blair Holt;
function photographs courtesy of Allen Carroll

"The main offensive action of [bagua] is the *Single Change.*
Indeed, it is more than that—it is the basic action in the art."
– Smith, 1967: 132

Introduction

This chapter analyzes a fundamental movement of *baguaquan* (eight trigrams boxing)—or *baguazhang* (eight trigrams palm), often abbreviated *bagua*—the "martial art," or what Donn Draeger calls the "civilian self defense system." Historically, bagua has no known battlefield record, so it cannot definitively be called a "martial art." According to its own legends and oral history, bagua originated among the anonymous Daoists of the mountains of Jiangxi Province. And Qing Dynasty (1644-1912) imperial bodyguards were known to have used it.

1

Bagua means "eight trigrams" or "eight warps." The character for trigram, pronounced "gua," originates from the word for the transverse thread on a loom. The meaning is much the same as the Sanskrit word *tantra*, which means "to weave." Although this term's philosophical depth is beyond the scope of this article, three horizontal lines symbolize the concept of bagua. This symbol also appears in Indian Samkya philosophy and is one of the ancient indications of possible Indian and Chinese philosophical syncretism. The upper line represents the order of heaven, the middle line represents the order of the human, and the lower line represents the order of earth. This three-fold aspect is not unique to the Chinese and is found in many ancient cosmologies. Bagua is about the interplay between these forces and how they can be aligned in a person. Bagua's self-defense system classifies its movements and principles according to this theme, using the trigrams and their eight combinations as an ordering system for movements, postures (static positions), and fighting tactics.

Since its popularization in the 1800's, bagua has split into many schools and there are many "masters" espousing exclusivity and "secret teachings." Some of the better known schools in the public view are those descending from reputed bagua founder Dong Hai-quan's students Sun Lutang, Yin Fu, and Cheng Tinghua. The Gao Yisheng lineage claims to have descended from a line parallel to Dong Haiquan. There are also bagua schools that have absorbed other kinds of boxing into their system like the "Drunken bagua" of Master Fu Zhensong, whose students, whose students presently teach in Shanghai.

To grasp the character of bagua's many variations is difficult, if not impossible. However, something can be understood from looking at the core form common to the many styles. This core movement is the "single palm change" (*dan huan zhang*). In this article, the author hopes to show five variations of this movement and, in doing so, expand the reader's awareness and discernment of what defines the self-defense art of bagua. The author has studied with lineage students of these five styles and is acutely aware of the dangers of misrepresentation. Still, paralysis may be worse than analysis, so let's take the plunge, realizing that these movements have not been derived from books or videotapes, but have been sweated over for some twenty years.

The Mother Palms

In bagua, the fighting tactics, anatomy, and esoteric teachings are organized into the same octagon, with eight hand movements, the *muzhang* ("mother palms"), corresponding to the eight phenomena. These "palms" are blended into a series of movements done while walking around a circle. There is a divergence of teaching on how the mother palms are performed. Some lineages turn their body and go the other way around the circle when they do a mother palm, while others change palms without changing directions. Still others teach the mother palms with arms held in static positions while walking the circle.

Depending on the lineage, other movements besides the mother palms are also taught. According to Chinese boxing tradition, empty hand training is followed by the study of standing locks and twists (*qinna*), vital points and resuscitation methods, and then weapon study. There is no groundwork or floor grappling. At present, most bagua boxing

2

is not taught very systematically and tactical functions are not emphasized.

Whatever the bagua boxing lineage, they all share two techniques: the single palm change and the circle walking exercise. The single palm change has variations and is classified differently in various bagua schools. Some lineages classify the single palm change as a primer for the more advanced Mother Palms. Other lineages consider the single palm change the first mother palm. Either way, the single palm change is the basic technique of bagua boxing. It is a way of changing the guard or leading hand and contains an arsenal of options for evasions, deflections, pulls, arm locks, strikes, and clamps to the head and body.

Circle Walking

The other basic bagua practice, circle walking, is the same between lineages. There are various ways to step on the circle and various circle sizes, but the walking basically remains the same.

Though circle walking is emphasized in bagua, it is not unique to it. Other Chinese boxing and ancillary skills of Dong's time, methods like *bapanzhang*, Sun Bin boxing, and *qinggong* (agility skills), used circle walking in their training. It was known as "gyromancy" in the British Isles, and the "Circle of Narvaez" in Spanish swordsmanship. Turkish wrestlers practice in a circle and in the Hindu religion devotees still circle around trees (as it is said Dong learned it). In ancient Greece, Melancomas circled his opponents, keeping his face unmarked by other boxers, a feat recorded in an essay by Chrysostom. Around the world, folk dancing has circled since ancient times. For these reasons, it is probable that more than one kind of circling body art for fighting and meditation was around during Dong's time. However, it was Dong's art in particular that was known for circle walking. Some schools favor one type of step over another. Most schools' teachings advance to a figure eight pattern and then work up to the circling of nine stations or posts.

Single Palm Change Variations

In this overview, four lineages and five variations of the single palm change will be shown. The reader can compare them through practice. When other writings appear on other bagua methods, they will have a basis for study and be able to see the range of movement allowable in the bagua entity—that is the deep underlying structure common to all lineages. The approach is similar in studying languages: first the standard forms are studied and from that the dialects can be appreciated.

The following lineages will be looked at:

A) Cheng Tinghua (?-1900) (via Sun Lutang to the Zhang brothers, to Guo Fengchi, to Robert W. Smith). This version of the single palm change is found in Sun's text, *Study of Bagua Boxing* (1916). It uses more movements than other versions like those shown in the later texts of Huang Bonian and Gong Baotian. The other versions of the single palm change shown here also use fewer movements, omitting the final toe-in or combining the first two arm movements into a single movement.

B1–2) Li Cunyi (1849-1921) [via Chen Panling to his sons, Yunqing and Yunchao]. There are two variations shown for these: one from each of Chen Panling's sons. The range of movement of the younger son's version contrasts strongly with the compactness of the older son's.

C) Zhang Zhaodong (1858-1938) [from Wang Sujin to Robert W. Smith and Marnix Wells]. Within the same alignments as the Li Cunyi lineage, this version shows an emphasis on the edge of the hand and use of the elbow.

D) Song Changrong (?) [via Gao Yisheng (1866-1951) to Zhang Junfeng, to Hong Yimian]. This version, the most compact style, is closest to that found in Huang Bonian's text *Dragon Shape Bagua Palm* (1936).

Each of these lineages is traceable to Dong Haiquan (1797-1882). The fourth lineage, that of Song Changrong, may have influences outside Dong. Dong popularized bagua boxing during the last century as the Qing emperor's bodyguard. There is speculation as to how much of bagua boxing Dong created and how much he learned. Dong claimed to have learned bagua from a Daoist (some versions of the story say two Daoists) in the Jiangxi mountains. Revisionist historians on Mainland China claim Dong invented the bagua system from his own synthesis of Daoist circle walking and Shaolin or Lohan boxing. The justification of this theory is odd, even lacking documented evidence of Daoists teaching a circular boxing to people at that time. After fifty years of social-political destruction, it is absurd to demand evidence from a group of Daoists hermits specializing in anonymity. Bagua, and Chinese boxing in general, has always been an oral tradition. Only since the early part of this century has there been substantial writing on them. Some of this century's best writing and research on martial arts, including many works by Chen Panling, were destroyed during the Cultural Revolution (1966-76).

However, oral traditions have been among artists and craftsmen since time immemorial. These traditions are often considered "secret traditions" not because they should be kept from people, but because only the practitioners of a school will grasp the nuance of a teaching. You have to experience it to understand it. The saying, "Only show your poems to a poet," contains the same idea. Observers may think there is a secret hoarded away, but practitioners have experiences from long practice. Common experience is an important part of the teacher-student relationship.

Comparing The Single Palm Change

The single palm change begins from an orthodox guard position with the left palm toward the center of the circle as one walks counterclockwise on the circle.

First Phase: The Toe-In — Cheng's single change begins with a ninety-degree toe-in and a turn of the waist leftward, putting the hands on the perimeter of the circle. Li's begins with a less than ninety-degree toe-in (the feet form the same shape as the Chinese character for "eight"), but does not swing the hands to the perimeter. Notice the wider variations in stance and arms.

4

I-A) Cheng's version turns the waist rightward, drilling and swinging the right palm back toward the center, accenting the horizontal plane of movement. The left hand follows near the right elbow and is also drilling and swinging. The right step onto the circle is done with the movement of the right palm.

I-B) Li's version forgoes the drilling of the hands to swing back to center in a quick and short chopping action. The right step onto the circle is done with the chopping right palm. In the variation, drilling is amplified vertically by lifting the palms high and extending the right leg.

I-C) Zhang's single palm turns the waist rightward and swings both palms up while using the right leg to hook downward, accenting the right toe. Then, as the practitioner walks, the palms are brought to the center of the circle.

I-D) Song's version emphasizes drilling upward with the right fingers as the right foot steps out, gradually swinging the palms to the circle's center as the practitioner walks.

These five single palm changes from four lineages show the same action done with variations in range of movement and articulation of the hands and feet. They show the change of direction during circle walking with the arms aligned vertically over the legs during the crucial points of balance in the movement. These alignments are known as six harmonies (*liu he*) and they correspond to functions of the mind as well as limb alignments. The "six harmonies" are a defining characteristic of bagua boxing and other *neijia*, or inner school, disciplines, including xingyi and taijiquan. These alignments are:

> 1) **Hand over foot** – harmonizes air (*qi*, "air" is the direct translation, meaning rhythmic vitality).
> 2) **Elbow over knee** – harmonizes will (*yi*, "will" or "intention").
> 3) **Shoulder over hip** – harmonizes the heart (*xin*, "heart" pertains to both the organ and emotion).

The first two physical alignments do not exist during circle walking as the hands are pressing toward the circle's center and the feet are moving along the perimeter. This trains the person's will and body to balance and endure some contradictory feelings in the body. The physical alignments occur during the single palm change and the other changes. These alignments optimize leverage and defensive ability.

Varying the degree of toe-in and toe-out can change the single palm change's angle of attack. The diameter of the circle determines how much to toe-in or out. Zhang's version also begins with the toe-in, but does not separate the hands. Song's version begins with the toe-in and the arms begin to wrap around the body. This is similar to Huang Bonian's single palm change in his 1936 text.

Second Phase

2-A

2-A) then turns the left thumb down and toes the left foot out along the circle, pressing the right palm forward from underneath.

2-B) separates the hands as the left foot toes-out or steps out. Notice the palm variations and the variation in length of step and extension of the arms.

2-C) is very similar to Li's (B) version, the main difference is the articulation of the left palm as the left foot steps out.

2-D) takes the left foot out laterally, off the circle. (Stepping onto the perimeter is an easier, but not preferred, variation).

Third Phase

3-A) toes-in the right foot, taking the right palm around the waist to turn up under the left elbow while the left hand turns palm up at head height.

3-B) shows two variations in this phase, bringing the right foot to toe-in or suspend it at the ankle. The former allows better action in the hips. On either step, the right palm is brought around the waist under the left elbow. The left palm keeps its articulation but follows the torso.

3-C) brings the right foot to suspend at the left ankle. It also keeps the left arm well extended and aims the right fingers underneath the left armpit. This is the most compressed arm action seen in these variations.

3-D) also suspends the right foot and takes the right palm under the left elbow as the left hand turns palm up at head height. The wide left step out and off the circle positions the practitioner with his back to the circle's center.

3-A

9

Fourth Phase:
Various Functions of the "Swing Back"

"Swing back" is essentially the same in these lineages. The underlying palm and the leading leg move back along the circle, the hands swinging to the center in one step, or one can continuously walk along the circle slowly raising the hands and lowering them to the center in one-and-a-half revolutions around the circle. The functions for the Swing Back can vary with arm and leg extension as with a taller opponent (see picture of the Li single change where I kick and break the arm) or timing (notice the immediate application from circle center with the Gao single change.) The swing back can also use the forearm across the diaphragm, swing into the opponent's rear arm, or be used to grab his throat.

4-A

4-BI

Teachers agree on the single palm changes' importance in teaching decisiveness. The emphasis is on decisive and crisp energy while completely changing direction. It shows a change of guard from one side to another and embodies the quality of *metanoia* (Greek for "turning," sometimes translated as "repentance"). In this way, the single palm change is in accordance with both Eastern and Western schools of esoteric/spiritual teaching.

Major Features of the Single-Palm Change Functions Sun Lutang Version

1. As the attacker targets my head from the rear,
2. I toe-in and turn to deflect with my left forearm.
3. Then I toe-out my left foot and roll my left forearm up to press his elbow upward and outward,
4. While pushing or striking his left ribs with my right palm.

5. Then, I toe-in my right foot, checking his left knee, while catching his left wrist with my left palm-back. My right hand comes under my left elbow and my right humerus comes under his left humerus.
6. I can use my right shoulder or right arm to impact his left elbow or humerus for a break.
7. Then, while he's off-balance, I swing back quickly with a right forearm to the diaphragm (8).

Chen Yunqing Version

1. Here, my expansive left arm "flapping" action (like a backhand) is used to engage a taller opponent.

2. I then lower his left arm by pressing down with my left wrist, while swinging my right arm to feint to his throat or break his elbow and lift my right foot to kick his rear knee or genitals.

Chen Yunchao Version

3. After the first toe-in, I toe-out and, with a compact swing of my left palm, I pull his elbow aside slightly, turning his body to expose his ribs.

Wang Sujin Version

Here, my extended chop on the single change is used to take my opponent's wrist and pull him enough to expose his side and cancel out the punch from the other arm. My right hand, elbow, or shoulder can then be used to target his obliques, armpit, or ribs. I can lift my right foot used to protect my left leg against his right kick (not shown). Note the angle of our bodies.

Gao Yisheng & Zhang Junfeng Version

1. Beginning from the left circle walk, I engage the opponent's left arm.
2. I slide up his incoming left by pressing it down to my right palm.
3. I then toe-in my right foot, continuing to guide his left punch by my body while I palm his chin. The opponent's forward momentum should bring him into the palm strike.
4. I can also lock his left arm by bringing my right arm under and around his left arm. My "tiger mouth," thumb and index finger crescent, surrounds his left wrist. The shadow in the photo obscures it, so look carefully.
5. Keeping my lock on him and my left arm up, I then step out and back with my left foot about ninety degrees, and continue the lock to carry my opponent around me.
6. Then I toe-in my right foot to whirl my opponent's head down in line to strike him with my left hand. [In photos 6 and 7, the technique is demonstrated from the opposite angle].
7. I then release my right arm lock to grab my opponent's throat. Note that at the same time I lower my left arm to trap his left arm.

Conclusion

From the above examples, the reader should be able to discern the chief physical characteristics of all bagua styles: 1) All walk the circle as a training exercise. 2) The primary defensive position (the arms) is basically the same in circle walking, though expansion of the arms varies. 3) The six alignments are maintained between the heart (*xin*)–shoulder-hip; intention (*yi*, will)—elbow-knee-*qi* (synergistic energy); and hand-foot. 4) The torso is held vertically throughout the walk and the single palm change movement.

The six alignments keep the body configured for easy defense and mechanical advantage. Bagua optimizes effort through mechanical advantage. Basic leverage as embodied in the six alignments is the foundation technique of all the various energy (*qi*) theories in Chinese boxing.

The bagua shown here eschews flamboyance for efficiency and attempts to reduce all tactics to walking and turning. Using the waist as the axis of movement and supporting the hands and arms through the back and legs, bagua is a manifestation of the whole body in movement, moving from strongly reinforced positions in a circle.

Bagua is a civilian self-defense system. Principally, armed escorts and convoy guards used it during the Manchu incursion. It was first made public by Dong Haiquan (1797-1882), who demonstrated it to the emperor at a banquet. Through Dong's students, it branched into approximately five styles that have been modified, improved, and deconstructed. There is controversy over styles that have suddenly been "rediscovered" in the Peoples' Republic of China. It seems the martial arts' commercial aspect and the tourist trade have spurred this trend.

Some systems seem more whole or systematic than others. Some have merged with other forms of "boxing." Some have become more physical education oriented and have lost their tactical meaning. All the systems hold the core of circle walking in their training and emphasize proficiency in walking and turning (i.e. the single palm change). The author hopes the reader will now have a grasp of what bagua is about and have a basic picture in mind when contrasting it with the study of other martial arts styles.

Bibliography

Huang, P. (1936). *Lung xing bagua (Dragon shape bagua palm)*. Shanghai.

Smith, R. (1967). *Ba-kua: Chinese boxing for fitness and self-defense*. Tokyo: Kodansha International.

Sun, L. (1916). *Baguaquan xue (Study of bagua boxing)*. Beijing. Reprinted in Hong Kong in 1960.

Glossary

baguaquan	八掛拳	Jiangxi	江西
baguazhang	八掛掌	Li Cunyi	李存義
Chen Panling	陳泮嶺	qing gong	輕工
Cheng Tinghua	程庭華	Song Changrong	宋長榮
dan huan zhang	單換掌	Sun Bin Quan	孫臏拳
Dong Haichuan	董海川	Sun Lutang	孫祿堂
Gao Yisheng	高義盛	Wang Shujin	王樹金
Gong Baotian	宮寶天	Yin Fu	尹福
Guo Fengchi	郭鳳墀	Zhang Zhaodong	張兆東
Huang Bonian	黃栢年	Zhang Junfeng	張俊峰

Special thanks to
Chris Martin & Jason Connelly for
their help in the technical section.

chapter 2

Yin Style Baguazhang
Hidden Treasure of Chinese Martial Arts

by James Smith, Ph.D., with Matt Bild, Translation

He Jinbao, in the classic dragon guard stance, working with Matt Bild.
Applications photographs courtesy of Andrew Nugent-Head.

Introduction

The Japanese martial arts of karate, judo, and aikido have been widely practiced in the West for decades. Korea's taekwondo has also become familiar to Western practitioners. The Chinese Shaolin *gongfu* styles have been seen in the action films of Bruce Lee and Jet Li. Also, the Chinese internal art of taijiquan ("grand ultimate fist") has become popular, both as a martial art and for its health and meditative benefits.

By contrast, China's *baguazhang* ("eight trigrams palm") is not all that widely known or appreciated in the West. Yet among knowledgeable Chinese practitioners, baguazhang is ranked as one of China's most sophisticated and effective styles. Like its better-known relatives taijiquan and *xingyiquan* ("mind-form fist"), baguazhang is an internal style that emphasizes mind and energy work as much as physical development, even from the earliest stages of training. It is also the youngest of the major Chinese arts, dating to the second half of the 19th century. The first man to openly teach baguazhang—and in all likelihood, the art's creator[1]—was Dong Haichuan (1804-1880), a gifted martial artist whose stature in his day could perhaps be compared to that of Morihei Ueshiba, the creator of aikido, in the 20th century.[2] Like aikido, baguazhang's late development enabled its creator to draw on a wide range of existing arts to create a synthesis that strives to surpass its models.

19

Even among baguazhang practitioners, the Yin style is relatively little known. Although Yin Fu (1841-1909) was Dong Haichuan's first and most thoroughly taught student, his style is but one among several schools, and by no means the most widespread. Cheng Tinghua's (1848-1900) style is more widely practiced both in China and the West. This is largely because Cheng was a prolific baguazhang teacher, whereas Yin taught only a small number of students, and passed the entire system to only Men Baozhen (1873-1958).

It would be a futile and tendentious exercise to speculate about which school is the most martially effective, the clearest embodiment of baguazhang's Daoist philosophical roots, or otherwise "best." As a purely historical observation, however, the Yin style has a particularly strong claim to reflect the breadth of Dong Haichuan's baguazhang practice. This is simply because Yin Fu spent far more time under Dong's direct tutelage than any of his other students.

In comparison with other styles, the sheer volume of material in Yin Baguazhang also argues for its proximity to the art's source. Inferences from such factual and historical observations are complicated, however, by the fact that advanced baguazhang practitioners are expected to adapt what they have learned to their own strengths and circumstances. Thus, both Yin Fu and Cheng Tinghua—as well as the other great practitioners whose lineages survive to our day—certainly altered what they learned from Dong.

Exactly what Dong Haichuan taught is lost in the proverbial mists of time. Even among those schools that can validly trace their lineage to Dong, several generations of alterations—both intentional and otherwise—have taken their toll. That said, one modern baguazhang school with impeccable historical credentials is the Yin Fu lineage, through his disciple Men Baozhen (1873-1958), to Men's disciple Xie Peiqi (1920-2003).

Left: Xie Peiqi (1920-2003), third generation Yin Style Baguqzhang lineage holder, and teacher of He Jinbao. Right: Xie Peiqi, performing the dragon system's chopping attack.

This chapter will present this challenging baguazhang school to the Western audience, largely through the insights of one of the style's top practitioners. He Jinbao (b. 1955), Xie Peiqi's designated successor. One of Beijing's most respected martial artists, Mr. He works to disseminate Yin Baguazhang in Europe and the United States. In addition to providing an introduction to the style, Mr. He provides a glimpse into a martial arts milieu rarely viewed by Westerners, and rapidly disappearing in modern China as well: a world where teachers tested students' dedication by demonstrating violent or painful techniques on them, and where friendly disagreements about the martial efficacy of different styles quickly resulted in challenge matches.[3]

The Four Pillars of Practice: Striking, Standing, Circle-Walking, and Transitioning[4]

Owing to its breadth, depth, and complexity, Yin Baguazhang is a difficult art to pin down. It would be wrong to characterize it as a kicking/striking style like karate, taekwondo, or Thai boxing, even though it has an enormous repertoire of kicks and strikes. Likewise, it would be incorrect to class it with the grappling styles such as judo, *shuaijiao* (Chinese wrestling, "throw-wrestling"), and aikido, despite its frequent use of close-quarters locking and throwing techniques. Yin Baguazhang also includes healing and qigong systems that are considered separate from the martial system. It is an art defined by principles rather than techniques.

According to He Jinbao, the essence of Yin Baguazhang as a martial art can be summed up in three words: precise, vicious, and cold. Together, these connote an art that can be extremely brutal, yet which relies upon accuracy, skill, and intelligence in application, rather than brute force.

Baguazhang is not only a fighting art, it is also a system of comprehensive self-development. He Jinbao lists four basic goals that the serious baguazhang practitioner should strive to develop simultaneously:

• **Strength:** This refers primarily to the development of the muscles and connective tissues. In this sense, baguazhang can be considered a sophisticated form of physical exercise—one that works the muscles and connective tissues in a more deep and complete fashion than popular Western exercises such as jogging, aerobics, and weightlifting.

• **Health:** This refers to improvement of the functioning of the internal organs, and to energy development.[5] Accomplished baguazhang practitioners are noted for maintaining youthful vigor in their old age, as well as for their fighting skills.

• **Fighting:** This refers to the ability to apply baguazhang to practical martial ends—whether in competition, in a self-defense situation, or on the battlefield. Like most of the classical Chinese fighting arts, baguazhang was initially developed for practical combat use by soldiers, bodyguards, and caravan escorts before the diffusion of firearms in China.

- **Aesthetics:** Performed correctly, baguazhang is pleasing to both the eye of the onlooker and the aesthetic sense of the practitioner. However, Yin Baguazhang is emphatically not a "performance art" in the style of modern wushu routines: every movement has practical utility in the health, strength, and martial dimensions; the aesthetics emerge as epiphenomena of correct practice.

To achieve these four ends, Yin Baguazhang relies on four basic pillars of practice. The first is striking, which is perhaps the easiest to grasp. A Yin Baguazhang hallmark is the repetitious practice of basic strikes drawn from the system's 64 attacking methods (each attacking method is based on a principle of movement with numerous deflecting, grappling, and striking applications). Strikes are drilled in a wide variety of stepping patterns, including but not limited to stationary drilling; straight-line stepping; four-corner (box) stepping patterns; and the signature Yin "three-step method," which combines sweeping, hooking, forward stepping, and backward stepping movements in a challenging but concise pattern. He Jinbao insists that the key to developing practical martial power in Yin Baguazhang is endless repetition of simple striking drills, particularly on a straight line.

The second pillar—familiar to taijiquan and xingyiquan practitioners, but baffling to many other observers—is the standing posture (*zhanzhuang*). This practice involves holding a series of stationary postures to strengthen the body both internally and externally. This is particularly helpful in developing internal energy, tendons, and muscles. Unlike taiji standing, in which postures are held in a deeply relaxed manner, the Yin Baguazhang standing postures emphasize precise isometric force. He Jinbao notes that, when done correctly, these postures will never feel entirely comfortable, no matter what the practitioner's development level. This contrasts with the striking, which gradually becomes more comfortable as the practitioner gains skill.

Left: Lion smashing entry—direct and aggressive, dominating the opponent's force (pure yang).
Right: Unicorn—soft and flowing, transforming the opponent's force (pure yin).

The third pillar is circle-walking,[6] a simple but profound practice common to all baguazhang lineages. Like standing, this type of walking appears esoteric to the uninitiated; it involves walking in a circular pattern while holding one or more fixed upper-body positions, and occasionally changing direction. Accomplished baguazhang practitioners sometimes walk for considerable periods in a single practice session; an hour or more is not uncommon. In mythic renditions of Dong Haichuan's life, it was said he circled around a tree for so long that the trunk began to bend toward him! Although circle-walking has major benefits in the health, strength, and fighting dimensions, some of these benefits are difficult to grasp without first-hand experience in circle-walking. On a simple physical level, this walking improves the practitioner's balance, stability, stamina, and concentration. On the applied level, it develops an instinctual feel for moving to an opponent's flank and avoiding force-against-force encounters in fighting situations. On a more esoteric level, advanced practitioners derive meditative and internal-energy benefits from circle-walking practice. So, despite its superficial simplicity, circle-walking is also the deepest baguazhang practice. While all four pillars are given equal emphasis at the beginning and intermediate levels, circle-walking assumes greater importance as the practitioner progresses to higher levels.

The fourth pillar is transitioning, which is closely intertwined with circle-walking practice. To transition from clockwise to counterclockwise walking (or vice versa), Yin Baguazhang teachers have created a huge repertoire of short combat routines. These routines link strikes into useful combinations, meld different attacking energies, and develop sophisticated stepping skills; they will look vaguely familiar to practitioners of striking/kicking arts that emphasize standardized practice routines. The routines are not set in stone; the changes that He Jinbao teaches to his students are not identical to those he learned from Xie Peiqi, and more advanced students are, in principle, free to create their own changes.

While the precise details of particular transitions are not fixed, however, the overall system of transitions follows an explicit taxonomy in which strikes, steps, and attack energies are combined in clearly prescribed ways. There are 448 distinct transitions (64 attacking methods times seven variations per attacking method) in the taxonomy. Correctly executing even the seven changes for a single attack method can be the work of months or years, although learning new changes tends to come more easily with time. Not surprisingly, few practitioners—even the most advanced— attempt to master anything like the complete set.

The Animal Systems

Yin Baguazhang is organized into eight sub-systems, each derived from a trigram of the Daoist classic the *Yijing*, and associated with a representative animal. Yin Baguazhang's immense repertoire of strikes, steps, internal energies, and external forces is systematically constructed from the animal building blocks. This emphasis on the animal systems differentiates the Yin Baguazhang of Men Baozhen and Xie Peiqi from other baguazhang schools, most of which place little or no emphasis on separate animal systems.

In this taxonomy, one animal is pure *yang* (hard, strong force), one is pure *yin* (transforming force), and the other six are combinations of yin and yang. A very brief summary of the animals and their distinctive personalities follows:

- Lion system (*qian* trigram) is pure yang—vicious, linear, and direct. It is a particularly effective system for building external strength. Like xingyi, it attacks by aggressively cutting through the opponent, adopting the defensive only for tactical purposes. Its overwhelming force allows the opponent no time or space to recover and counterattack—a principle known as interlocking in Yin Baguazhang. "Interlocking" is sometimes translated as "interconnecting," as the Chinese word implies the continuous application of attacks. In the lion system, however, these are not separate attacks in rapid succession, but rather attacks that fit into each other (interlock) for increased efficacy.
- Unicorn system (*kun* trigram) is pure yin, and thus the opposite of the lion— soft and flowing, the embodiment of pure transforming force. It attacks by turning the incoming force of the opponent against him, a principle known as reversing the body. If the lion is the cocky prize fighter of baguazhang, the unicorn is the little old lady with a gun in her purse: not inherently aggressive, but quite capable of dealing with those who mistake softness for weakness.
- Snake system (*kan* trigram) embodies the principle of moving with the force—it wraps itself around the opponent at close range, attacking with joint locks and precise strikes to vulnerable points.
- Dragon system (*zhen* trigram) embodies the principle of lifting and holding— it controls the opponent by crowding his center, controlling his arms, and forcing him off balance, then enters with direct strikes to finish the fight.[7]
- Bear system (*gen* trigram) embodies the principle of turning the back— it specializes in attacking from an attitude of apparent weakness or retreat, often with close-in body blows that utilize the shoulders, back, and hips.
- Rooster system (*li* trigram) embodies the principle of the lying step—it dodges incoming attacks by moving the whole body, and counterattacks from a low, rooted stance.
- Phoenix system (*xun* trigram) embodies the principle of the windmill— it dodges incoming attacks with quick movements, then counterattacks with a flurry of rapid, whiplash strikes to vulnerable areas.
- Monkey system (*dui* trigram) embodies the principle of enfolding—it specializes in leg techniques including, but by no means limited to, kicking. As the term "enfolding" suggests, Yin Baguazhang often uses the legs to trap and unbalance the opponent, rather than to kick.

While each animal is a separate and complete martial system, each incorporates elements of the seven other animals. This is true even of the extreme yin and yang animals.

qian	kun	kan	zhen
gen	li	xun	dui

Historically, instruction in Yin Baguazhang was somewhat *ad hoc*. Beginners were typically given a set of techniques to practice (sometimes drawn from several animal systems), with no explanation of how these fit together.

Today, the preferred way to learn Yin Baguazhang is to pick an animal that is suited to the practitioner's psychological or physical make-up and achieve some degree of proficiency in it. This provides a foundation upon which the practitioner gradually incorporates elements of the other animals' personalities and martial repertoires. A high-level Yin Baguazhang practitioner can fluidly combine techniques and energies from all eight animals. He Jinbao emphasizes the need to achieve a thorough grounding in a single animal system as a foundation for further development. Partly, He's switch to this more systematic approach has been in response to his recent experience teaching students in the West, who do not have the luxury of absorbing the system over years of weekly classes in Beijing.

In terms of practical training, each animal system is associated with eight attacking methods, a characteristic stepping pattern, nine standing postures (a representative posture and one standing posture for each attacking method), and 56 changes (seven variations for each of the eight attacking methods). It is through executing the transitions within the circle-walking that the personalities of the other seven animals are integrated into the practice of a given animal. For example, the dragon system's eight attacking methods are:

- Pushing: a horizontal linear force
- Lifting: an upward linear force
- Carrying: a long two-handed pulling force
- Leading: a short one-handed pulling force
- Moving: a downward force with the back of the hand
- Capturing: a downward force with the front of the hand
- Chopping: a downward force with the palm
- Entering: a direct inward force preceded by an opening movement.

Each of these attacking methods has innumerable applications and variations. For each attacking method, there are seven changes, each of which incorporates the energy and personality of one of the other animals. Thus, for the first attacking method in the dragon system, there is a pushing/interlocking change (through which the personality of the lion enters the dragon system); a pushing/moving-with-the-force change (snake); a pushing/turning-the-back change (bear); a pushing/windmill change (phoenix); a pushing/ lying-step change (rooster); a pushing/reversing-the-body change (unicorn); and a pushing/enfolding change (monkey). Through practicing these changes, a dragon practitioner gradually becomes comfortable with the personalities and energies of the other animals. This learning process can be augmented by the judicious drilling of the basic strikes from the other systems.

There are supplementary practices in Yin Baguazhang outside of the eight animals taxonomy, which can be incorporated into the practice of any animal. These include a sophisticated system of joint manipulation and locking, kicking techniques, weapons drills and forms, and two-person applications drills.

As this brief introduction should make clear, Yin Baguazhang is a complex system that requires a sustained commitment from its practitioners. At the same time, however, its structure is highly systematic, allowing the practitioner to avoid getting lost in the overwhelming mass of material that it contains.

INTERVIEW WITH HE JINBAO
conducted on September 3, 2003 in Essex Junction, Vermont.

MARTIAL ARTS BACKGROUND

• **What makes Yin Baguazhang unique? What is its "essence" as a martial art?**

As a fighting art, Yin Baguazhang is cold, precise, and vicious. In terms of development practices, I believe Yin Baguazhang is the most complete style I have seen in my thirty years of practice. It simultaneously develops strength, health, fighting skill, and grace in motion.

• **Does Yin Style Baguazhang differ significantly from the more widespread Cheng Style?**

Cheng and Yin styles are quite different in many respects. For example, Yin style is known as "hard hand" and Cheng style is "soft hand." Yin style has natural stepping, and Cheng style has mud stepping, or the sliding step. Yin style has the small circle, and Cheng style has the large circle.

Also, in my view, Yin style has remained more focused on fighting applications, while Cheng style has put greater emphasis on forms. Of course, this depends on the individual practitioner. Whichever style you practice, it is important to be familiar with the other.

• **How did you first become interested in martial arts in general and baguazhang in particular?**

To be honest, I did not understand anything about baguazhang or the martial arts when I started. I did not put any real thought into what I was doing, because I was young—fifteen years old.

My first teacher was an elderly neighbor who started to teach me out of gratitude, because I had visited him when he was in the hospital. People told me that this old guy had a lot of skill, but I did not understand what they meant. It was through my first teacher that I met Dr. Xie Peiqi.

When I first started practicing, I just wanted to look good and be strong. At the time, weightlifting and fitness equipment were not widely available in China, and there was little in the way of organized sports. By contrast, martial arts were widespread, and were a practical and cost-effective form of exercise. All you needed were a few feet of empty space and you could get a good workout.

So truthfully, when I started, I was not thinking about how my practice would develop. It was only as I learned more that I became interested in the martial arts in themselves.

• **Your teacher, Xie Peiqi, had a reputation as both a colorful character and a tough teacher. Could you briefly discuss your first encounter with him?**

The first time I met Dr. Xie, he looked me over like a piece of meat, and said: "You'll practice lion." Then he showed me a lion form very quickly and perfunctorily. Remember that I was fifteen years old and had no previous exposure to baguazhang. I had no idea what he had done. But I did not dare to question Dr. Xie. It was very different from the situation today, when young people see movies and read books before they start martial arts training and will ask their teachers anything. So, I stood there dumbfounded, and the doctor said: "Well, come on, let's see you practice."

I just stammered: "I didn't really see what you did."

The doctor sighed and said: "Alright, I'll do it one more time." And he did it again—exactly like the first time; very quickly and without explanation. And of course I still did not follow it.

The doctor saw that I still did not comprehend, so he said: "So you're that stupid, are you? Okay, then I'll show you how to use this." In a few seconds, I was lying on the ground, and my first lesson was over. I still did not understand what the doctor had shown me—but he had had enough, and he went back inside to drink tea.

Clearly, there were large cultural differences between the environment when I started to practice baguazhang and the situation in the United States today. I think somewhere in between these two environments is best.

• **Dr. Xie was notorious for being very physical with his students, although much less so after he started to teach Western students in the 1990's. Do you ever strike your students?**

I've been teaching students at all different levels, and there are a number of reasons why I would strike them.

To be perfectly honest, the first reason is that I don't like you, and I would be happy to see you leave. The second is to wake up students who are not putting in a reasonable level of effort.

The third and most important reason is to demonstrate to a student how to apply something in a fighting situation. Some aspects of baguazhang cannot be easily conveyed in words, and must be experienced to be understood. If I strike students for this reason, I'm actually doing them a favor. Coming to a physical understanding of some technique early on will probably save them from greater injuries in the long run, if the alternative is to figure things out through trial and error in training and fighting.

If you study baguazhang or any martial art, you have to accept that you will get some cuts and bruises in your training. That's an unavoidable part of the process. You'll get cuts and bruises from your classmates if you don't get them from your teacher.

Classic High Transition—
leading the opponent high and entering low.

• **What is your view of wushu performances?**

This is just another aspect of martial arts, and a different kind of achievement. It's a good way to popularize martial arts. If you want to see a good martial arts performance, you must see the Beijing Wushu Team—no one even approaches them. On the other hand, if you want someone good at push hands, you should find a top taiji practitioner, because they are the best at push hands. Different groups excel at different things.

It is true, of course, that when you consider martial arts performers from the perspective of fighting, they are usually somewhat lacking. This is not to say that none of them could fight if they had to, but that's not what they stress, and that's okay. It works the other way, too: the guys who participate in serious fighting competitions—like, say, Thai boxers—wouldn't look very good in a performance venue.

Countering a grab—
with a characteristic twisting and locking technique.

REGARDING TRAINING

• **Is weapons training necessary for achieving a high level of skill?**

It does not matter whether you are talking about Yin Baguazhang or any other martial system: if you want to achieve a high level of skill, your training must be complete. Practicing with weapons is a part of this, although beginners must reach a certain level of skill with empty hands before moving on to weapons.

Practicing with weapons improves strength, timing, coordination, and general skill—including skill with your bare hands. After practicing with weapons, you will find your empty-hand techniques are more smooth and coordinated.

You might be able to get to this point without weapons—but weapons practice will get you there that much more quickly. Developing skill through weapons training is like taking medicine when you have a cold: eventually, you would feel better without medicine. So why bother with it? ... So you can feel better more quickly....

Consider the baguazhang large saber [approximately five feet in length and over seven pounds in weight]. Forget about practicing forms with it; for the average person, it is difficult just to pick up! Working with such a weapon will strengthen your hands and wrists, and will accelerate the development of your seizing and grasping (qinna) skills.

In my view, it doesn't really matter which weapon you practice; the specific weapon and its techniques are not the point. Rather, you practice weapons to hasten the development of your basic skill. You don't need to know a dozen different weapons forms; better to just pick one, and work at it.

Which weapon should you choose? In baguazhang, the saber is the signature weapon, just as the straight sword (jian) is the weapon of choice for taiji practitioners. But if the saber does not interest you, you should follow your own interests.

From a self-defense perspective, however, it makes sense to put a lot more time into your empty hand practice. After all, no matter which weapon you practice, there will be times when you don't have it with you! The only things you can't forget to bring with you are your hands.

• **How does Yin Baguazhang's strength development compare with Western strength training, such as weightlifting?**

When I first started with baguazhang, weightlifting and other strength-training equipment barely existed in China; they were just being introduced from the Soviet Union in the 1960's and 1970's. When I started working at a wood factory, we assembled some crude weightlifting equipment.

However, a lot of the older generation said that if I really wanted to be serious about martial arts practice, I should avoid weight training. They warned that weightlifting causes muscles to become short and contracted, which is not what a martial artist needs. Baguazhang, by contrast, tends to lengthen and stretch the muscles while strengthening them. So while it may not develop large muscle mass to the same degree as weightlifting, it does more to work the tendons and connective tissues.

• **Could you give us your thoughts on the role of the mind in internal martial arts training?**

In your practice, you must bring mind and body together; that is what complete practice means. This is why it is so difficult to reach a high level—you must have understanding as well as practice time.

Further, if you want to live for a long time, I believe you must have a positive attitude when you train. You have to have some spirit in your heart, and you must not dwell on the negative thoughts. You must keep your mind calm and focused when you train.

I've seen champion athletes who are not healthy people. It is not just exercise that brings health and longevity, and it is not just the physical body that matters. In baguazhang, you develop your mind along with your body; as your physical skills develop, so does your understanding and your wisdom.

We all live in an imperfect world. In this world, there is sickness, death, greed, anger, addictions. I believe that if you can remove your mind from these bad things through your practice, then you will live a longer and healthier life. I'm not talking about retreating to a mountain top to meditate, or physically removing yourself from society. I'm talking about the attitude you adopt in your training. It has to be positive and joyful. You cannot dwell on all the bad things, or get caught up in the pursuit of riches or success.

REGARDING FIGHTING SKILLS

• **The conventional wisdom is that most fights end up on the ground, so you have to be able to fight there. Yin Baguazhang does not explicitly train ground fighting, so how can it be used against a good ground fighter? Should Yin Baguazhang fighters cross-train in ground-fighting styles?**

It may be true that many fights end up on the ground; but all fights start standing up!

In the United States, Bruce Lee and those like him made Chinese boxing popular. Then the Brazilian Jujitsu guys came along and popularized grappling and ground fighting. But you have to realize that these are just two different methods. In either one, the key to success is to be good at what you do. You want to know about all the different methods of fighting, but you can't practice them all at once, because the different methods have different requirements—different rules for doing things correctly, so to speak.

Baguazhang large saber—He Jinbao with the saber,
over 5 feet in length, 7 pounds in weight.

31

Spear and large saber—Ed Guerra of Phoenix,
Arizona, demonstrating baguazhang weapon forms.

• **A lot of martial arts teachers argue that training for fighting competitions creates bad habits if your goal is realistic fighting or self-defense. What is your opinion?**

Real fighting is very different from competitions. In a competition, they are always looking to protect the competitors from serious injury or death, to some extent: you can't gouge eyes, you can't kick knees, whatever. In some cases, they will wear padding or gloves. There are always rules. That's what makes it different from a real fight in the street. In competitions, you are not literally fighting for your life; in a street confrontation, you may be.

There is a saying in Chinese that "all the training in the world is not as good as a real fight." People with a lot of experience in real fights will be good at fighting, just because they know what to expect.

We could also talk about the difference between fights that you see in movies and real fights. In films, they want a long fight that is visually entertaining. In real life, a fight doesn't last very long, and it is a lot uglier than those you see in motion pictures. Just look at the way they talk in movie fights: they talk in a calm voice, rather than screaming out obscenities, which is what you are more likely to see in a real fight.

• **A lot of martial artists think a lot about fighting and have theories about fighting, but real challenge matches are practically a thing of the past. You clearly have been in a number of challenge matches that could have resulted in serious injury to someone. Was this more common in China when you were learning? Do have any thoughts or anecdotes to offer on this issue?**

When I was first practicing in the 1970's, there were a lot of opportunities to mix it up with people from other schools and styles. But people were not really looking for trouble; they were testing their skills. There were a lot of people practicing a lot of different styles; you would look at what they did and they would look at what you did, and someone would say: "Okay, that looks interesting, let's see if it works...."

It was not simply brawling, or even going out there to prove one style was better than another. The attitude was one of testing your skills against—and learning from—others who had different skills.

Over the years, I've had a lot of people who wanted to test their skills against me. In fact, some of my best students are people who came to test their skills against me, were beaten, and said: "Hey, this works very well; I want to study baguazhang with this guy."

Another important aspect when I was learning was the opportunity to watch other people fight. There was a saying then that "one who stands on the sidelines has a clear view." If you are fighting someone yourself, frankly, you are not necessarily going to know everything that has happened. But if you are watching two other people fight, you can calmly analyze each move and technique—missed opportunities, moves that were not quite executed correctly, different ways of entering in on an opponent, and so on.

Left: lion-to-rooster transformation attacking low.
Right: dragon carry application.

REGARDING TEACHING & LEARNING

• **Do you believe the quality of martial arts instruction and practice are lower than they once were?**

It would be correct to say that in all the martial arts, we tend to see fewer people who are proficient at the highest levels today. This has to do with differences in both teachers and students today.

First, the teachers. I've seen many teachers whose development is extremely good, but they just can't teach very well. For some of them, this is because they are at such a high level that they only want to teach advanced material—even though most of their students cannot understand such instruction.

Another aspect is that a lot of the teaching methods that come down from the past are not applicable to modern times.

Second, let's look at the students. Students today practice for different reasons than they used to. Today, practicing martial arts is a hobby for most students. In the past, people who practiced martial arts were usually after a livelihood—they wanted to be bodyguards, soldiers, or whatever. This difference alone is bound to have an enormous effect on the development of the martial arts.

Also, a lot of students are not very realistic about learning a martial art. Many people today want instant results. They come to class like a fisherman with a hook, hoping to extract as much information as quickly as possible from their teachers. Such students may practice hard in class, but they do not follow up with their practice on their own time. They do not grasp the time and commitment that go into learning an art well.

And of course, students today are subject to many changes and stresses that affect their practice: they might get married, get a new job, have children. If you are busy with work, the children are screaming at home, and you can't find time to practice, of course that will affect your development.

On the other hand, there are some very positive developments today in the martial arts. Martial arts are becoming a kind of international sub-culture. There are international competitions and workshops, and teachers travel the world to bring their styles to others. In the past, you just studied with a local teacher in someone's backyard.

• **How do your experiences teaching in the West compare with your experiences teaching Chinese students?**

I feel there were three major milestones in my development as a martial artist: starting to study with Dr. Xie; having the opportunity to learn from Liu Feng[8] and other older, high-level practitioners in Beijing; and coming to Europe and the United States to teach.

Back when I started, teachers would show me things and I would go off to practice, but no one was concerned to make sure I was doing it right, or to explain why things were done one way and not another. But that's not the best way to learn, because you spend a lot of time making mistakes that have to be corrected later.

When I started teaching in Europe and the United States, I quickly discovered that students there expect more. I have to be accurate in my teaching and make sure everyone is getting it right, because that's why people in distant nations come to me to learn.

This has helped me, because if I'm not doing something quite right, Western students will pick up on it and ask me about it. For example, if one time I have my hands a little higher and the next time a little lower when demonstrating a strike, or if I step slightly differently when demonstrating a change on two separate occasions, they will ask me why I did it that way, and whether one way is more correct. I have to be able to explain these things. Maybe these are acceptable variations within a general principle, or maybe it is something with me that I have to be aware of—my development is not perfect. Or maybe I will show someone how to do something, and when they demonstrate for me I will think: Is that really what I taught them? Is that how I am doing it? Teaching is a great mirror on your own practice.

• **In your teaching, you stress patient effort over a long period of time as the key to success. Could you please elaborate on this?**

The Chinese characters *gongfu* literally mean "skill accumulated over time." If you practice martial arts and you wish to get real skill, you need time. Even good styles have practitioners who are awful, and even inferior styles have superior practitioners. A lot of it comes down to what individuals put into their practice.

It is said in China that you must practice a technique a thousand times before you really get it. Think about that—if you practice a technique every day, this means about three years before you understand it. So forget about learning eight animals, learning just one or two is a huge endeavor. I am amused by those who promise to convey high-level skills in a weekend seminar. If such a thing exists, sign me up; I don't care what it costs!

Phoenix sequence—dodging and striking.

35

Bear, Turning Back Entry— attacking
from a position of apparent weakness.

Snake finish—wrapping and
locking the opponent at close range.

36

- **When you first started studying Yin Baguazhang, you had some extraordinary teachers, and many highly proficient older practitioners around. Your foreign students generally do not have these resources. Does this put them at a serious disadvantage in learning?**

Not necessarily. The more important issue is personal commitment. Are you really willing to spend a lot of time practicing this art? Are you willing to ponder what your teacher tells you, and figure out what it means for yourself? Are you willing to really put some time and thought into assessing your own progress, and identifying the areas where you need more work? Are you willing to spend time looking at other styles, analyzing their strong points and learning from them?

It is not a question of the people you have around you, it is a question of what you are willing to put into your practice. The more you practice and ponder, the higher your practice will become. You have to dive into this study completely, with real commitment. If you are willing to do this, you will be successful.

Notes

1 A few baguazhang schools claim a lineage that predates Dong; see for example Liang, Yang, and Wu (1994). However, according to Miller (1994), martial arts historian Kang Gewu's exhaustive investigations into baguazhang's origins failed to produce convincing evidence for such claims. There is no doubt, however, that Dong's baguazhang drew heavily from existing martial arts and Daoist practices.

2 In Chinese internal martial arts circles, the two 19th-century practitioners who typically rate comparison with Dong are taiji master Yang Luchan and xingyi master Guo Yunshen. All three are credited with skills that dramatically surpass those of modern-day masters.

3 In a friendly match, victory was traditionally decided by a knock down or first blood, although concerns about "face" often led to rematches that were decided only when one person was no longer able to fight. Less-than-friendly matches frequently ended in serious injury, and occasionally even death.

4 In addition to drawing on He Jinbao's personal insights, this section draws upon several introductory works on Yin Baguazhang cited in the bibliography, especially Andrew Nugent-Head's excellent essays on the Association for Traditional Studies web site (www.traditionalstudies.org), Richard Miller's articles in *Tai Chi Magazine* (April 2002 and October 2003), and Dan Miller's *Bagua Journal* articles on Xie Peiqi and Yin Baguazhang (November/December 2003).

5 He Jinbao prefers not to confuse beginning students with discussions of energy work (*qi*). Accordingly, this article will refrain from further exploration of this concept.

6 Circle-walking (literally, "turn the circle") is a term typically used in English writings on baguazhang, and is used here for clarity.

7 Cheng Baguazhang emphasizes the dragon character of Yin Baguazhang. It is, therefore, likely that Cheng Tinghua's six years of instruction with Dong Haichuan focused on this animal, in contrast to the more eclectic instruction received by Yin Fu throughout his longer association with Dong.

8 One of Dr. Xie's senior students, who clarified much of Xie's sometimes cursory instruction for He.

Bibliography

Liang, S., Yang, J., and Wu, W. (1994). *Baguazhang: Emei Baguazhang*. Boston, MA: YMAA Publications Center.

Miller, D. (1994). Yin Fu's Ba Gua. *Pa Kua Chang Journal* 4(1): 3-15.

Miller, D. (1994). Xie Pei Qi's animal forms. *Pa Kua Chang Journal* 4(1): 16-22.

Miller, D. (1994). The circle walk practice of Ba Gua Zhang. *Pa Kua Chang Journal* 4(6): 3-22.

Miller, R. (2002). Yin Style Bagua Zhang. *T'ai Chi* 26(2): 31-40.

Miller, R. (2003). He Jinbao on bagua turning. *T'ai Chi* 27(5): 28-34.

Nugent-Head, A. (n.d.): "Understanding Yin Style Bagua," downloaded from the Association for Traditional Studies website (www.traditionalstudies.org/ysb/understanding.html).

Acknowledgments

The author would like to thank the following individuals without whose generous contributions this chapter would not have been possible: Arthur Makaris, for reviewing an initial draft; Brad Pettengill, Richard Miller, Ed Guerra, and Steve Brooks for providing photos; Matt Bild, He Jinbao's tireless student and translator, for posing for the applications photos and translating the interview; and, above all, Andrew Nugent-Head of the Association for Traditional Studies (www.traditionalstudies.org) for providing the applications photos and editing the article in detail.

chapter 3

How Baguazhang Incorporates Theory from the *Book of Changes*

by Travis Joern, B.A.

Photography by Christian Lamothe.

Introduction

The Chinese martial art style known as baguazhang is a northern style that is unique because of how it identifies the *Yijing*, otherwise known as the *Book of Changes*, as the source for the theoretical principles used in training. The style has branched off into various schools, as the records in its history seem to point out that many students were instructed on not being too rigid about a specific pattern of training, but adapting the training toward their own abilities once they had learned the fundamentals. The goal of this chapter is not to examine the specifics of any particular branch or school of thought within baguazhang, but to examine how a martial artist can make use of a book such as the *Yijing* and try to determine why baguazhang practitioners chose this particular text as the core of their training. Three possible uses of the *Yijing* will be explored here: first, as a means to understand Daoist conceptions of the body and how it functions within the world; second, as a source of moral guidance; and finally, as a philosophical approach to combat strategies. Regarding to why they chose the *Yijing* as opposed to other sources of material, the answer proposed here is that by associating themselves with the *Yijing*, the teachers of baguazhang are able to link their style of training to the cultural prestige placed upon the text.

39

The Book of Changes

The *Yijing* was used for a wide range of applications throughout history. Some saw it as a book of divination, or even a piece of sacred scripture, while others have described it as being "a book of philosophy, a historical work, an ancient dictionary, an encyclopaedia, an early scientific treatise, and a mathematical model of the universe" (Smith, 2008: 1). It could be used simultaneously in various domains, such as astronomy, geography, music, strategy, phonology, and mathematics (Smith, 1993: 13). It was seen as a way of determining one's place in the scheme of things by learning how the *dao*, or the way of nature, was configured in moments of cosmic order (Lynn, 1994: 1).

There was the belief that the *Yijing* had within it the wisdom of a "superior man," where thoughtful meditation on its images and judgments could impart wise decisions for one's course of action within any situation (Wilhelm, 1997: 68). Casting and divination worked from the idea that everything that occurs within a given moment "is interrelated and that all such events somehow share in the same basic character" (Lynn, 1994: 18). The *Yijing* represented the relationships and processes at work within the cosmos, and not only could these relationships be known, but an understanding of them could be used to determine effective action within human society (Peterson, 1982: 85).

There are four main claims about the *Yijing* as a source of wisdom. First and foremost, it is interpreted as a microcosm of the universe, through which one can study the patterns and relationships that occur in nature. Second, these patterns and relationships are revealed in the hexagrams, trigrams, and lines of the *Yijing*. Third, the *Yijing* presents to those who use it a "potent, illuminating, activating and transforming spirituality (*shen*)." The forth claim is that by exploring the wisdom hidden within the *Yijing*, "one can discern the patterns of change in the universe" and thus not only know fate (*zhiming*), but even establish fate (*liming*). As such, it was seen as an effective guide for one's actions through the changing circumstances of life (Smith, 2008: 38).

In the story of its creation, the *Yijing* was seen as something produced from nature rather than being the artificial fabrication of man (Smith, 2008: 191). While it is difficult to determine the factual history behind the development of the *Yijing*, the commonly accepted story is that Fu Xi[1] studied the patterns of heaven, earth, and man together, and mapped them out as the eight trigrams (Peterson, 1982: 68). These trigrams were then combined in pairs to map out the different relationships that occur in nature, which formed the 64 hexagrams. King Wen of Zhou (r. 1171–1122 BCE) (Lynn, 1994: 4) added upon these hexagrams the explanatory text known as the hexagram statement (*guaci*), or judgement (*tuan*), attaching a line statement to each individual line (*yaoci*) to help with the interpretation of the readings of the *Yijing* (Smith, 2008: 9). The final major attachment to the canon of the *Yijing* was the "ten wings," which was supposedly added by Confucius.[2]

There were different modes that one could use to read the *Yijing*. Some popular methods included treating the hexagrams as pictorial representations or icons, which inferred that they were representations of physical elements of the world and revealed its subtler processes. Another method looked for the relationships that could be discerned between the lines of the hexagram, where combinations revealed certain aspects of the reading. Some readings also looked at hexagrams as a relationship between the traits of two trigrams, and looked to how they could be interacting (Smith, 1993: 10).

One popular reading looked at the structure of a hexagram as breaking down the various elements of any given situation. The first line (from the bottom up) described its beginnings, and the second marked the height of its internal development. The third line described a moment of crisis within the situation, while the fourth marked an external aspect. The fifth line was seen as the highest point of development, and the sixth related to a completion, or even an overdevelopment (Smith, 2008: 29).

The commentaries on the *Yijing* are influenced by a rich combination of Confucian, legalist, Buddhist, and Daoist views, with cross-referencing essays and drawn-out debates that occurred over the centuries. It was constantly reinterpreted by different thinkers, where even famous neo-Confucian writers such as Zhu Xi (1130–1200 CE) added to the selection of readings to draw from (Lynn, 1994: 7). Some saw it as a cosmological text that gives insight into the intricate workings of the divine in nature. Others saw it as a book of wisdom that allowed one to navigate complicated social relationships. Later scholars even saw it as a mathematical codex, through which all patterns could be learned and all of existence broken down to numbers and formulas. Divination practices and reading the *Yijing* would often be acts performed in privacy, as in traditional society it could be a great loss of face to discuss hardships openly, and government officials often did not have the luxury of saying "I don't know what to do" when the emperor asked for their council. The competition among scholars in the imperial age was such that their "workspace" was an environment in which their peers would constantly be trying to cause them to lose favor in the court, or even to humiliate them publicly.[3]

41

A strong aspect of the legitimization of sovereignty in classical China was derived from the Mandate of Heaven, so a series of mistakes that caused problems for the people could be construed as a sign from the heavens that the time in office had expired for those in power. Not only was it important to learn how to conduct yourself according to the cosmos, but it was also a lifesaving skill to know how to point out that even when times are bad or the situation is inauspicious, you are still in a position of virtue, and in accordance with heaven and earth, so you would be able to point out that it was not your fault in the first place. Historically in China, many dynasties have been overthrown by rebellions driven by the ideal that the emperor in power had lost the Mandate of Heaven. While there are, of course, other factors involved in such regime changes, claiming the Mandate of Heaven was an incredibly powerful method of recruiting people to your side and increasing the size of your armies in classical China.

The summary of this is that the *Yijing* has been a text credited with great value throughout a very long part of Chinese history. It was seen as a mysterious and powerful book in which you could find any answer, if you knew how to read it properly.

A Short Introduction to Baguazhang

Turning now to baguazhang, the main focus of this chapter, let's first look at what it was as a system or style of martial arts. The theories behind the foundation of baguazhang are varied, where the creation of the system has been attributed to different masters and different circumstances. Typically, this creation story shifts according to which branch of the bagua system you study under, as different teachers attribute it to the masters they are more familiar with. In his book, Jerry Alan Johnson lists four possible stories, and others could be included as well. However, as with the *Yijing*, the origins of baguazhang are not the objective of this study; rather, we are trying to understand how the two were connected.

Regardless of variations, one of the people most commonly credited with the development of the style is Dong Haichuan (1797–1882 CE). Whether or not he was the true founder, he still remains one of the most important figures for the style in the nineteenth century, during what are believed to be the early years of the compilation of baguazhang. Practitioners assembled training methods from different systems of martial arts, many of which were connected to histories of the Shaolin and the Wudang mountains.[4] While the circular training format was most commonly attributed to a Daoist meditation exercise, the belief is that bagua represented an amalgamation of what Dong Haichuan saw as the most useful aspects of different martial arts systems.

Dong Haichuan was a servant who became a martial arts teacher in the imperial palace. This rare case of social mobility could only be attributed to outstanding skill.[5] The story of his promotion took place at a particularly crowded banquet, where he impressed the emperor with his agility and dexterity in navigating through the crowds while carrying plates of food. At one point it was claimed that he even ran along the wall to bypass a throng of partygoers (Johnson, 1984: 3). Working as a martial arts teacher within the palace would have been quite an improvement over being a mere servant or even a guard forced to stand at attention throughout the day. Competition for the position would have been fierce,[6] and Dong Haichuan would have had to prove his mettle against some of the greatest fighters within the imperial army.

Baguazhang was seen as a fighting system suited for the "learned man," as its foundations were claimed to be derived from ancient philosophical beliefs, and its teachings were guided by ethics (Vargas, 1983: 8). One of the concepts driving this emphasis on education and morality was the fact that being able to survive violent encounters was not simply a matter of defending oneself in combat. More important, it is the ability to anticipate the circumstances that lead up to a fight, and to know how to secure the advantageous position within any confrontation. Survival also extends into the way in which one navigates social relations, particularly in the ritual-bound interactions of imperial China.

The emphasis on ethics in baguazhang served many purposes, one of which was to try to safeguard the teachings from unethical or overly ambitious people. It was the task of the master to determine and refine the moral quality of his students, only teaching the true secrets of the style to those who would use them responsibly, knowing that once knowledge was imparted unto the student, it could not be taken back.

The nature of baguazhang as a style of fighting was similar to that of taijiquan and xingyiquan. The three styles together are often referred to as the *neijia*, or internal family. Bagua centers on palm strikes,[7] evasive footwork, and body mechanics which emphasize dynamic changes. The movement is designed to develop agility and swiftness, with strong power in the legs which allows for freedom and control of movement. The goal of training for the practitioner was to reach not only a high level of physical conditioning, but also to learn methods that help to maintain a state of relaxation in both the body and the mind while fighting. "With a relaxed body, the flow of blood will not be impeded, and the muscles will not be tense, thus allowing the body to move naturally" (Johnson, 1984: 12).

There are different levels of training found within bagua. The most basic are external skills (*waigong*). These are the visible aspects of any style of martial arts, such as strength, agility, coordination, flexibility, and balance. Though they are seen as the least complicated level of training, this does not mean they are easy to learn. Many drills under this category are incredibly difficult and take years of training to perform properly. It is believed that without strong development in these fundamental skills, the student cannot properly develop the following levels.

The next level is that of internal skills (*neigong*). This training emphasizes the development of secondary muscle groups, ligaments, and tendons that people are not usually able to consciously control.[8] The objective in this level is to cultivate a relaxed form of movement that can still generate striking power and speed, working toward a refinement of mechanical alignment in movement. The third, more advanced level is that of *qigong*,[9] which deals with breath control, visualization, and body movements ultimately designed to align and harmonize the flow of energy within the body (Johnson, 1984: 3). The qigong techniques used in bagua are believed to be the Daoist contribution to the style.

In learning bagua, the concept is that the students are not simply learning a series of movements in a form: they are expected to learn principles and methods behind the creation of these movements. Learning the form in and of itself is a nice exercise in coordination and memory, but without the principles behind it, it is nothing more than a series of gestures. There is a very deep study of movement that must occur for the student to develop the ability to not only apply the forms in fighting situations, but also to be able to adapt and change the movements as needed depending on the circumstances of the fight.

The principles used in baguazhang are not only physical, but also based on tactical and strategic methods of combat. The purpose of applying bagua is to be able to respond, adapt, and change in a spontaneous manner (Miller, 1993: 26). Proficiency is not simply being able to properly execute movements in training; it is the cultivation of a high degree of reflexive responses. Through long, intensive training, students can create specific reaction formations that allow them to respond to the movements of the enemy while still being able to calculate strategic movements that can give them an advantage.

Not only must a student be able to adapt and vary his movements, he must do so while adhering to the principles of body mechanics within bagua which allow the student to generate the striking power to inflict structural damage on the body of his opponent. These penetrating blows target specific areas, such as joints, nerves, sinews, and organs, where a solid hit can stun an opponent long enough to create the opportunity to land a fatal strike if necessary (Miller, 1993: 5).

However, even though it employs attacks to targeted areas, bagua is supposed to work with a dynamic of movement that can be connected to the Daoist principle of *wuwei*.[10] The idea is not simply that of nonaction, but spontaneous action, which does not arise from a motive or seek a specific result. While there is the desired result of victory over the opponent, this is not achieved through a specific goal of striking him in the head or deliberately trying to grab an arm to do a joint lock. These actions are not supposed to occur through deliberate choice, but they should be performed through a type of sense that skilled fighters have to develop: where they try to feel out the opponent and react accordingly, rather than simply acting upon the opponent with the desire to use a specific strike. Victory should be obtained simply by moving through the necessary actions which result in the neutralization of the threat being presented. This being said, sometimes in confrontations, victory is simply realizing there is no real threat, and walking away.

Now, the idea of fighting without the intent of using certain attacks may seem a bit strange. In training, you prepare certain attacks and try to master specific strikes in a manner described above, where you seek out certain targets in the body. The notion is

44

that there is a step between training and fighting, wherein you do want to learn and refine certain attacks, but there is a critical element of training those attacks to the point where the response becomes more like a reflex than action. You want to open your awareness to the opportunities that present themselves within a fight, but in such a manner that you do not deliberate over what attack you should use. Instead, you simply attack the openings as they are presented and defend yourself as needed, in a manner that will reposition you into a stronger situation in the fight.

When a martial artist applies the concept of *wuwei*, it refers to a state whereby the fighter has knowledge of "principles, structures, alignments, rhythm, timing, optimum angles of attack and defense, and the economy of motion" (Miller, 1993: 27), but he does not try to deliberately apply any of this knowledge. The fighter must remain in a calm, clear-minded state, having a certain plan of action in mind, but staying ready to discard that plan to respond in a spontaneous manner to the movement of the opponent. The thing to understand here is that the ability to maintain a clear mind does not, and cannot, undercut years of intensive training. It is only a means to harmonize training into the most effective manner of application.

To try creating a visual of this, imagine yourself facing off with an opponent. In this case, imagine that you have decided to engage; that is, disengaging without combat is no longer possible. Essentially there are two actions one could take: wait for an opening and attack, or trigger a reaction in the opponent and respond based on the opponent's action. In either case your training has taught you not to focus on a specific action—a punch, a kick, or a throw—but rather on the geometry of the interaction, the shape of the space encompassed by you and the opponent.

Operating at this level of abstraction is what allows you to remain calm and centered—in wuwei—while simultaneously adjusting position. Suddenly the intention arises within you to attack, triggered by an intuitive recognition of opportunity. You begin to move forward and punch him in the left side of the face, but as you move, the opponent shifts to the right and kicks at you with his left leg. If you were too focused on the mechanics of punching him, you would get hit with the kick. But if you were able to remain calm and aware of the interaction, you would notice the opponent's movement and respond by shifting your body just far enough away from the arc of the kick to avoid the strike, or at least lighten the impact. This would allow you to trap the leg without injury or, alternatively, deliver a counterstrike that requires slightly less time to land than the kick. You would hit the opponent in a manner that destabilizes the structure of his body to diminish the power of the kick.

The cultivation of this level of skill and awareness, which few are able to fully master, requires many years of training. A quote that describes the difficulty of this says, "Of the ten thousand things in this world, two are particularly hard for man to reach: the moon, and proficiency in Chinese boxing" (Vargas, 1983: 8). Chinese martial artists often like to say that you need to "eat bitter" (*chiku*) in order to develop skill. This is not a phrase said in lighthearted jest. Bitter would be the taste of your teacher hitting you when he showed you how to block, long hours of difficult drills, and landing from countless throws and takedowns. Contemporary studies on expert performance predict that it takes about ten thousand hours of intensive training to reach a level of mastery in any sport or performance-based skill (Ericsson & Charness, 1994: 741). Martial arts are no different, and that adds up to a lot of bruises from misjudging what it takes to avoid an attack.

The *Yijing* as a Means to Understand the Body

Now then, having a better understanding of the *Yijing*, as well as bagua, how did the people who trained in bagua use the *Yijing*? As mentioned earlier, one of these possibilities was to examine Daoist conceptions of the body. If the *Yijing* was premised on the notion that all phenomena, all conditions, all processes, and all relationships in the world could be explained, then it seems a logical step that the *Yijing* could be used to explain the functions and processes of the body. The *Yijing* was indeed known for having strong connections to Daoist conceptualizations of health. This lies in the fact that Daoists saw the body as a microcosm of nature, and since the *Yijing* was used to interpret nature, it could therefore be used to interpret the body.

Fu Xi supposedly drew influence from both man and nature together to create the trigrams, so it was understood that the body and nature functioned together through the same processes (Smith, 1993: 5). As the prime elements of the cosmos were those of heaven, earth, and man, they were connected in various patterns of relationship and resonance, and the "circumstances of their being (and becoming)" were conditioned by the same patterns of movement and change (Smith, 2008: 35). This meant that all changes that occurred within nature also occurred within the body. Richard Smith mentions that enthusiasts of Daoist alchemy drew heavily upon the *Yijing* in their quest for longevity and eventual immortality (Smith, 2008: 106).

Scholars fond of Daoist teachings propagated some of their own developments in the understanding of the *Yijing*, where the system of the five phases (*wuxing*) was incorporated into some readings of the *Yijing*. This correlative system dated back to the Zhou Dynasty (1046–256 BCE), where the earliest combination was found in two tablets: the Yellow River Map (*Ho Tu*), and the Writing from the Lo River (*Lo Shu*), both of which were believed to have mythical origins. It is, therefore, difficult to pinpoint the historical date of their creation (Wilhelm, 1977: 81).

The five phase theory was central to popular conceptions of the body in traditional Chinese medicine that were derived from the Western Han (206 BCE-9 CE) cosmology of Dong Zhongshu (179-104 BCE)[11], where elaborate systems of correspondence and resonance were applied to conceptions of the body. The five phases were mapped onto different organs, and how they interacted within the constitution and functions of the body. "Internally, the body has five viscera, which correspond to the five agents. Externally there are four limbs, which correspond to the four seasons. [...] In what may be numbered, there is correspondence in number [*tongshu*]. In what may not be numbered, there is correspondence in kind [*tonglei*]" (Smith, 2008: 35).

While we could continue to break down the ways that the *Yijing* correlates with the body, at this point it would be safe to say that this information would have been useful to practitioners of baguazhang. It served as the basis for their understanding of the body and was an important aspect of the internal training they used to strengthen and condition the body, particularly their training which worked toward the harmonization of the qi within the body. Bagua practitioners incorporated traditional Chinese medicine into their training, using herbs and acupuncture treatments to improve the health of sickly students, and to repair the injuries that occurred within combat training. Some teachers even provided medical services to the public.[12]

The *Yijing* as a Code of Ethics and Moral Guidance

Even those who dismissed the mantric functions of the *Yijing* recognized its potential as a tool for moral cultivation (Smith, 2008: 175). In some examples, such as hexagram of *Lu*, "courage and foresight, determined behavior, and perseverance together with awareness of danger are necessary" (Wilhlem, 1977: 55). This shows how some predictions were formed in a manner that morality or virtue was crucial for placing oneself in the auspicious position where even an inauspicious reading could be salvaged by maintaining virtue and making wise decisions (Smith, 2008: 95).

As baguazhang was treated as a lifetime dedication, some students could end up learning many of life's lessons through the school. Their teachers didn't simply present fighting techniques, they offered the students instruction that could be used in every area of their lives. As much as it was the teacher's task to present the student with ancient knowledge, it was also the teacher's task to transmit morality and decorum. Students were members of the school, and therefore they represented it in the public sphere. The *Yijing* could thus be used as an instruction manual for these morals and guidance so the students themselves could explore teachings of wisdom and develop their own insights to pass on to future students.

Wang Bi (226–249 CE), a popular scholar who wrote on the *Yijing*, focused on issues of political and social morality (Smith, 2008: 94). He related the *Yijing* directly to concrete human affairs. Using the hexagrams as indicators of how one should respond to change, Wang Bi stressed the importance of flexibility in decision making. Understanding how chaotic the unfolding of events can seem at times, we could all probably think of some examples where people have met with hardships because of their inability to move with the changes that occur throughout life.

There is also mention of the idea of a moral, "Kingly Way" (*wangdao*), one exemplified by the regularities found in nature and symbolically manifested in the *Yijing*. This was derived from the concept of an ideal social and political order which was represented in the lines, trigrams, and hexagrams of the *Yijing* (Smith, 2008: 104). The Kingly Way was based on natural governance, which worked from the regularities and patterns found in nature and was manifested symbolically in the *Yijing*. Ruling according to the Kingly Way would allow officials to govern by wuwei, using moral example and ritual rectitude rather than laws and punishments. While this Kingly Way was intended for the rulers, it is plausible that those who studied it would try and find to ways it could be applied to their own lives.

Other thinkers, such as Yuan Jian (1141–1226 CE), saw the *Yijing* as a reflection of the self, where the mind was equivalent to nature, and changes could be related to innate virtues of the mind (Smith, 2008: 137). This meant that the study of the *Yijing* could allow one not only to learn how to benefit from divinations, but also allowed the common man to develop the mental virtues he could carry with him through life. He could develop the wisdom and clarity that could see him through calamities and become a role model for the people he met and interacted with.

The Potential of the *Yijing* for Combat Strategy

While the elements of training in bagua that focussed on harmonizing the body and cultivating morality were essential for the growth and development of the students, baguazhang remained first and foremost a fighting art. As the *Yijing* was the theoretical groundwork for the style, it might be fruitful to also explore the potential of the *Yijing* as a guide for military strategy. There was the belief within the *Yijing* that "if one can determine which situation prevails at any given moment, what one's place is in that moment and situation, and how one relates to the other major players involved, 'Change will yield its all'" (Lynn, 1994: 16). This belief, though formed originally on the basis for effective action within the realm of human society, could be applied to a fight.

Within a fight, the options you have for attack and defense are based on the situation at hand and the positioning of those with whom you are fighting. You cannot simply charge in, but must learn to analyse the strengths and weaknesses within both yourself and the opponent, and what action is best suited for what situation. The main characteristic of a fight is constant change, where in each movement the situation changes, so effectiveness is based primarily on one's ability to be fluid and act in accordance with this change.

The *Yijing* looks at the totality of changing phenomena in terms of a structured law of form. This structured law of form could be applied to combat in order to create a systematic understanding of attack and devance. This could occur through an intensive study of how different movements open up the possibilities of different attacks or defenses. Examining distancing, speed, and placement of yourself and the opponent, you could determine which attacks would be effective in which situations.

This logical construction of a systematic process of fighting allows one to adapt quickly to changing situations. In his application of the *Yijing* to music, Helmut Wilhelm discussed the determination of form where the situation creates the theme. Theme here could be understood as the dynamic of movement in fighting. "No absolute limitation is imposed upon the freedom of the musical imagination in developing the theme within the frame of a definite form" (Wilhelm, 1977: 49). Though it calls for a bit of abstraction, this concept applies to fighting in the sense that one should enter combat in a clear state of mind, whereby the fighter does not try to force certain attacks or defenses, but allows the situation to define what action would be used for attack or defense. The closest possible union between imagination and form is the expression of a natural way through which the movement of the fighter flows naturally to position himself in relation to strengths and weaknesses—his and those of his opponent.

The principle here is both simple and infinitely complex. If you can clearly perceive and understand the present situation, what your place is in that moment, and how you relate (spatially, physically, mentally) to the others involved, "change will yield its all."

Some people enter a fight simply with the goal of hitting their opponent until he goes down. Sometimes the physical conditioning of such a fighter is good enough that such a simple strategy is effective. However, baguazhang was originally designed for use in real combat, where one should expect a match to end in the death of one of the combatants involved. There was an expectation that fighters could find themselves facing multiple opponents or exotic weaponry and fighting techniques they had not encountered before. In such circumstances, it would be dangerous to base your combat strategy on simply being stronger or faster than your opponent.[13] While you could recover from a surprise attack within a competitive match, this would not be the case when a surprise attack takes the form of a knife to the ribs.

The emphasis on training in bagua is on mobility and placement: where you cultivate the ability to move in any direction at any point in time. This allows you to place yourself strategically when having to fight against multiple opponents, where you can avoid becoming surrounded and attack in flanking movements that catch your opponents off guard, using arcs rather than straight lines to control range.

Change is described in the *Yijing* as something that is not carried out abruptly and irrationally. It functions through fixed points and a given order (Wilhelm, 1977: 23), and combat should be carried out in a similar manner. This entails a system of fighting that may appear random and chaotic while remaining inwardly controlled and decisive. It is through an in depth understanding of the patterns of movement, attack, and defense that you can navigate these patterns to prepare yourself for all possible encounters.

Cultural Prestige of the *Yijing*

Even though we've looked at some ways that the *Yijing* could be useful for martial artists, it would still be pertinent to ask why baguazhang practitioners chose to publicly identify the *Yijing* as the theoretical basis of their style of martial arts. To answer this question, a strong argument could be made that not only did the teachers of baguazhang want to benefit from the knowledge within the *Yijing*, but they also wanted to benefit from the reputation that the book held within the intellectual culture of Imperial China.

As a school of martial arts, the style of baguazhang not only had to compete with other styles to demonstrate the proficiency of its techniques in combat; it also had to compete with different methods of self cultivation. While practitioners wanted their training to remain secret and refrained from demonstrating attacks publicly, if they did not teach the style, it would have disappeared within a generation or two. While the tradition of teaching the next generation of your family was common, it was not guaranteed that you would have a child capable of, or even interested in, mastering a complicated form of martial arts. By connecting their style to something with as much cultural significance as the *Yijing*, bagua practitioners would have had something that helped raise the distinction of their style above those of other schools of martial arts, which would in turn attract promising students.

Today (particularly if the student comes from a North American background), the *Yijing* may seem like an obscure and exotic source of knowledge. However, in late Imperial China, when baguazhang was developed, the *Yijing* was a well known book (at least to the literate), being one of the four great classics of Chinese culture. The *Yijing* provided bagua practitioners not only with the lessons and insights seen as essential for any cultured "gentleman" of that time, but by connecting their methods of training with the esoteric nature of the *Yijing*, bagua practitioners formed what could be seen as a divine validation to the purity of their training.

Despite all the disagreements over how the *Yijing* could be used, the vast majority of intellectuals in China prior to the 20th century considered the *Yijing* a "document of unrivalled prestige and unparalleled scriptural authority" (Smith, 2008: 3). It was a text seen as essential for advice in times of personal, social, or political crisis. It was a source of metaphysical understanding of the world: even court officials used it in the midst of conflict and indecision (Smith, 2008: 6). Among scholars there was a sentiment that "solid scholars" confined themselves to narrow textual studies (*wenju*), while the "intelligent people" (*gao-mingzhe*) drifted into unrestrained and obscure cosmological teachings to develop profound insights (Smith, 2008: 162).

Wilhelm claimed there was an unwritten law, where "only those advanced in years regard themselves as ready to learn [the *Yijing*]" (Wilhelm, 1977: 3). Many people believed that the "ordinary man" could be guided by the *Yijing* to act in such a way as to become a "superior man" (Peterson, 1982: 85). The "gentlemen" of Chinese culture were those who were believed to possess profound knowledge of the cosmological processes of nature. When martial arts masters were looked up to by their students for wisdom and advice, the reputation of having learned the secrets of the *Yijing* would have positioned the bagua teacher as having a profound understanding of heaven, earth, and man. Knowledge of the cosmic changes were believed to refine one's "potency and achievements in human affairs" (Peterson, 1982: 91).

Of course, while this is an important dynamic to consider when looking at bagua as a school which needs to recruit talented students in order to transmit the knowledge through different generations, the goal here is not to cheapen the use of the *Yijing* as some kind of selling point. Some teachers made no effort to promote their teachings openly, and made students work hard to prove themselves worthy of training in baguazhang.

Above all else, the moral quality of the students and their dedication to the school would have been the critical aspect to deciding who could receive the inner secrets of the style. There are stories where students had to spend years proving to their teacher that they were worthy and capable of learning all the complexities of baguazhang. However, because the style was so complicated and took so long to learn, it was rare to find someone capable of completely mastering the art. When such students were so hard to find, certain steps had to be taken to create a reputation for the style which would draw quality students into the door. It is only through talented students that the style could survive and the full breadth of the teaching be transmitted to the next generation. It is possible that, by openly communicating the fact that bagua was linked to the *Yijing*, baguazhang instructors tried to raise its prominence as a style of martial arts. Do not forget that they could have hidden the fact that there was a connection to the *Yijing* and still have benefited from its use in training.

Application One (A)

1) Both fighters are squared off. **2)** The attacker comes in with right punch, while the defender steps off on a diagonal, piercing out to intercept the attack. **3a)** If the attacker doesn't offer enough resistance to the intercepting palm, one can continue in on his centerline to pierce the eyes or throat.

Application One (B and C)

1) Both fighters are squared off. **2)** The attacker comes in with right punch, while the defender steps off on a diagonal, piercing out to intercept the attack. **3b)** If the attacker does resist enough to stop the pierce, then the pierce hand can turn over into a grab and pull the arm down, as the other hand strikes the face and the back leg kicks the knee. **3c-d)** If the attacker is resisting a lot, come underneath his arm in the first move, to bypass his upward pressure, and then step in with the back leg as you strike down on the neck.

Application Two

I) Both fighters square off. **2)** Here the bagua fighter is going for a backhand strike with his leading arm. **3)** If the other fighter sees the opening, he can step diagonally into the strike for a kick to the ribs. **4)** If the bagua fighter is aware of this kick as the opponent starts to move, he can push off the lead foot to rotate himself outside of the arc which offers the kicking leg the heaviest amount of impact. After pushing off with the lead foot, the bagua fighter can use the training from a common bagua pose to protect himself. **5-a)** From there, he can step down and trap the leg if the other fighter is slow to pull it back, allowing a him to follow-up with a trip or throw. **5-b)** If the other fighter is already pulling back his leg, he can simply use the stronger positioning to kick out from the stance, aiming for either the solar plexus, hips or groin, allowing him to follow-up with other strikes or a take-down.

Conclusion

It might be important at this point to mention that this chapter is simply aimed at trying to form a better overall understanding of baguazhang and the theoretical work behind it. The ideas herein are not proposed as a concrete explanation of all systems of baguazhang. Even in the first generation of its transmission, Dong Haichuan was said to have instructed each of his main students on different aspects of training, emphasizing not some fixed understanding of bagua, but concepts to be applied to one's own strengths and weaknesses that worked from the fundamental training. This diversity carried through following generations of students, and today there exists a rich blend of styles within bagua that have different forms, exercises, and approaches to training.

Accepting that different schools of thought may have different interpretations on the details of training, it is hope that this chapter will encourage an exploration of the theoretical basis of baguazhang and the cultural context from which this theory was developed.

We can see that there were indeed some very insightful ways that martial arts practitioners could draw information out of the *Yijing*. Whether they wanted to learn of the cosmological principles that guided the functions of the body, if they needed some moral guidance in a moment of difficulty, or even if they wanted to expand on some of the combat strategies they developed from training, opening a copy of the *Yijing* would have been a beneficial practice.

The teachings of the *Yijing* often seem vague and difficult to interpret, but it is because of this that people were able to apply it to so many different fields of study. As one of the four classics, and a subject used in imperial examinations, there was no denying the prestige of the book. While baguazhang practitioners could have used its teachings in secret to develop the theories behind their training, they decided to openly promote their style as having its roots in the *Book of Changes*. In doing so, they benefited from its prestige, where people who had trouble deciphering the cryptic messages of the *Yijing* would have been quite impressed with teachers capable of developing an entire system of martial arts from the principles of the *Changes*.

Acknowledgment
Special thanks to Mitchel Macintyre (black uniform) for helping with this chapter.

[1] Fu Xi is an ancient mythological hero said to have lived in the mid-2800s BCE. He is reputed to be the inventor of such cultural necessities as writing and fishing, plus devised the eight trigrams to better live in accord with nature.

[2] Each of these claims of names and exact dates are debated, but unfortunately we won't be able to go into those details here. The true origins of the *Yijing* is a worthwhile debate, but not relevant enough to the main point of the chapter for anything more than a brief mention of the most commonly described story.

³ There are many tales of officials and scholars trying to outwit each other, some of which you can find in the *Spring and Autumn Annals of Master Yan* (*Yanzi Chunqiu*), believe to be writing in the Warring States Period (475–221 BCE).

⁴ It was a very common practice to link a system of martial arts to the famous mountains to add in the symbolic value of authenticity, as has been described in Meir Shahar's work in *The Shaolin Monastery* (2008). The Wudang mountain represented a connection to Daoist teachings on self-cultivation, and the Shaolin mountain would have offered a link to not only the reputation of Shaolin martial arts, but also their Buddhist teachings.

⁵ Moving from a servant to the respected position of a martial arts master within the imperial palace would not been easy. If Dong Haichuan did not have the legendary abilities attributed to him, he was quite skilled in negotiating imperial social relations. His tomb is located in an area strictly reserved for important figures of Chinese history, an auspicious spot which money alone cannot buy.

⁶ There was even mention of an Imperial wrestling team, the Shan Pu Ying camp, which trained vigorously and had regular competitions. Dong Haichuan would have had to possess skills to match the skills of these professional fighters, and justify his place among them as a teacher. Information on the Shan Pu Ying can be found in Ma Mingda's article (2009).

⁷ The basic palm methods are the single palm, double palm, colliding palm, piercing palm, provoking palm, overturning palm, swaying body palm, and revolving body palm (Johnson, 1984: 12)

⁸ This is because the muscles are not used often in the actions the majority of people perform throughout the day. Many of them are the 'core muscles' of the torso which control balance and posture. Modern systems of physical conditioning like Pilates work on similar same areas, though in different ways.

⁹ *Qigong* is a term which is notoriously difficult to translate, at its most basic level, it means breathing exercises, but it incorporates Daoist cosmological principles where everything in nature is constituted by qi. You are not simply breathing in air, but you are striving towards harmonizing the qi which constitutes your body through exercises that tonifies or expels various aspects of qi within the different meridians of the body.

¹⁰ *Wu* literally means to be without, and *wei* means action, doing, striving or straining for the sake of something. The most common translation is non-action, and wuwei is a term derived from Daoist philosophy.

¹¹ Dong drew from a variety of philosophical and religious traditions including those of the Yellow Emperor's concepts of medicine from the *Huangdi Neijing*, and the teachings of Laozi. His teachings of cosmology were commonly used in Daoist practices of physical and spiritual cultivation (Smith, 2008: 36).

¹² The majority of training manuals on bagua include lists of relevant acupuncture points to be used therapeutic techniques, and many also list herbal formulas to be used in conjunction with training.

¹³ Though of course you still trained to try and be faster, and learn to apply greater power in your strikes than anyone else.

Bibliography

Bracy, J. and Liu, X. (1998). *Ba gua: Hidden knowledge in the Taoist internal martial art.* Berkeley, CA: North Atlantic Books.

Farquhar, J. (1996). *Knowing practice: The clinical encounter of Chinese medicine.* Boulder, CO: Westview Press.

Gallin, B. (1978). "Comments on Contemporary Sociocultural Studies of Medicine in Chinese Societies," in Arthur Kleinman et al. eds., *Culture and Healing in Asian Societies: Anthropological, Psychiatric, and Public Health Studies.* Cambridge: Schenkman, pp. 173–181.

Johnson, J. (1984). *The master's manual of Pa Kua Chang.* Pacific Grove, CA: Ching Lung Martial Arts Association.

Liang, S., Yang, J., and Wu, W. (1994). *Emei baguazhang: Theory and applications.* Boston: YMAA Publication Center.

Lynn, R. (1994). *The classic of change: A new translation of the I Ching as interpreted by Wang Bi.* New York: Columbia University Press.

Obeyesekere, G. (1978). "Illness, culture, and meaning: Some comments on the nature of traditional medicine," in A. Kleinman et al. eds., *Culture and Healing in Asian Societies: Anthropological, Psychiatric, and Public Health Studies.* pp. 253–263.

Ma, M. (Summer,). "Reconstructing China's indigenous physical culture." *The Journal of Chinese Martial Studies,* Vol. 1, pp. 8–31.

Meir, S. (2008). *The Shaolin monastery: History, religion, and the Chinese martial arts.* Honolulu: University of Hawaii Press.

Park, B. and Miller, D. (1993). *The fundamentals of Pa Kua Chang.* Pacific Grove, CA: High View Publications.

Peterson, W. (1982). "Making connections: 'Commentary on the attached verbalizations' of the Book of Changes." *Harvard Journal of Asiatic Studies 42* (1) 67–116.

Porkert, M. (1974). *The theoretical foundations of Chinese medicine: Systems of correspondence.* Cambridge: MIT Press.

Shahar, M. (2008). *The Shaolin Monastery: History, religion, and the Chinese martial arts.* Honolulu: University of Hawai'i Press.

Smith, K. (1993). "The difficulty of the *Yijing.*" *Chinese Literature: Essays, Articles, Reviews,* 15: 1–15.

Smith, R. (2008). *Fathoming the cosmos and ordering the world.* Charlottesville, VA: University of Virginia Press.

Vargas, F. (1983). *Pa-kua: The gentleman's boxing.* Los Angeles: Vision Press Films.

Unschuld, P. (1985). *Medicine in China, a history of ideas.* Berkeley, CA: University of California Press.

Wilhelm, H. (1977). *Heaven, earth, and man in the Book of Changes: Seven eranos lectures.* Seattle: University of Washington Press.

chapter 4

Baguazhang in the Hong Yixiang Tradition

by Hong Dzehan (洪澤漢), with Christopher Bates and Robert Lin-i Yu

Hong Dzehan is flanked by those who have helped bring this piece to fruition:
Robert Lin-i Yu (translation) and Chris Bates (translation and photography).
All photos courtesy of Christopher Bates.

Where I Learned These Techniques

Of course I am biased, but even by others' accounts, my father Hong Yixiang (1925–1993), was one of the twentieth century's most notable teachers of Chinese martial arts. He gained fame in Taiwan as a fighting master of xingyi, bagua, and taiji, training students who won national tournaments in the 1970s. His skill was made known to the world by Robert W. Smith's pioneering Chinese martial arts books, and *The Way of the Warrior*, BBC's profile about him. His prominence was further spread in Taiwan, the United States and beyond by the many Taiwanese and foreign students he taught, such as Eric Luo, Su Dongcheng, Robert Yu, Mark Griffin, Chris Bates, Marcus Brinkman, and Abi Moriya.

My grandfather wanted his sons to have a well-rounded martial education and invited top teachers as they fled mainland China with the KMT to teach them. Among these teachers were Zhang Zhunfeng and Chen Panling. Both of these teachers saw the potential of my father and uncles and drilled them hard, seeking to prove that local Taiwanese could stand up to the best mainland fighters. This they did. Ultimately, my father and uncles each mastered their own specialties.

The passing on of a martial arts system from a father to his sons is a venerable tradition in China. My brothers and I were schooled intensely by my father and uncles and competed with each other for our father's attention through the training. After his untimely death, we continued to combine our knowledge and train with our uncle, Hong Yimian, until he died.

Memorable Incidents Involving These Techniques

As engendered in the lineage name—Yizong Cheng School Gao-Style Baguazhang, brought to Taiwan by Zhang Zhunfeng and passed down by Hong Yixiang (*yizong* meaning essence of change)—recognizes that change is an inherent element of combat between two opponents. Being able to change in response to an opponent, to adapt, is a fundamental skill in bagua. A higher level of skill encoded into the training sequences is to bring overwhelming change to the opponent, change that attacks his very ability to adapt to it. I coined the term *3D fighting* to describe this. Bagua forms anticipate several responses from the opponent, and to each response bagua has an answer that leads to further control over the opponent until he is defeated. Typically, this control is established by manipulating the opponent to his very core. Through such techniques as locking up limbs, breaking balance, and blinding, we disrupt his ability to adapt to change.

On one occasion thirty some years ago, I was sparring in the old school with one of the senior students famous for his very mobile and fluid xingyi style. It was an "ah-ha" moment for me when I was able to get bagua's indirect stepping and overwhelming change to work for me. We were both suited in the chest protectors designed by my father that allowed heavy contact. My opponent was very mobile and fast, difficult to attack frontally. I circled to his right outside and controlled his right arm, punching repeatedly low and high into his chest. Six blows landed as I drove him back. Finally, he jerked back the arm I had controlled, turning his body into the action and launching a left cross. I was able to adapt to this change, ducking under and parrying his strike over my head, twisting his body, unbalancing him at the core, and shoving him off balance. It was one of those moments that feel like magic as he just sailed away uncontrollably.

Tips on Practicing the Techniques

Bagua sequences embrace change, prepare the practitioner for change, and fundamentally target the opponent's capacity to adapt to change. Practice the form alone, then with a partner. A key element is "bridging"—to close the measure with the opponent and make contact with his guard. With a partner, practice making the initial bridging technique from different sides and angles. Learn to make the bridge and follow-up technique quickly and smoothly, keeping in mind that sometimes you slow the technique down in order to elicit the response you want from the opponent.

Techniques: Yanking Palm and Searching Palm

Two of the techniques in the first set of sequences—yanking palm and searching palm—are typical. They start with the same technique used in many other sequences to establish contact with the opponent (1a–c), but diverge depending on opportunity. Simultaneous with a step to the outside angle facing your opponent, your leading hand wraps and pulls down on the opponent's opposite hand, a move that seems to "open the door" for him to strike (1b). If he strikes with the available hand, your next move blocks it with a piercing palm from the outside angle (1c).

The piercing palm converts to a grab while the leading hand now abandons its attachment to his opposite arm and flows up to launch a second piercing palm (1d). If he blocks with his free hand, grab that as well.

From this point there are other bifurcations in the attack that could lead to other sequences—for example, searching palm (1a–c+2d–e). You stand outside of the opponent, close the protective gate, transfer the first piercing-palm hand to the opponent's arm, and jerk his arm across his body, breaking his stability at the core. This is like pulling the wound-up string on a top. However, just at the moment when the opponent might start to adapt to the direction of the jerk, you change the course, yanking his momentum and body down, and then in the opposite direction (1d–e). The coup de grace of the sequence is a double palm strike cum push (1g–f).

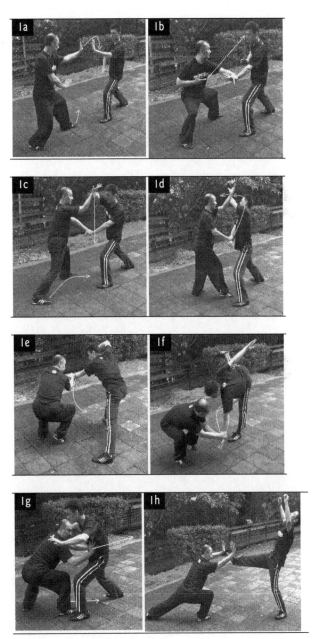

Alternate follow-up.

chapter 5

Some Insights into Xingyiquan:
Interview with Luo Dexiu

by Dietmar Stubenbaum and Marcus Brinkman

Mr. Luo Dexiu in a dragon posture.
All photos courtesy of D. Stubenbaum and M. Brinkman.

The following interview was conducted on October 17, 1993, in Taipei, Taiwan. Its contents convey some thoughts elicited during a lengthy interview with internal martial arts teacher Luo Dexiu.

- **How should one begin the practice of xingyi?**
  Although each style of xingyi may have characteristics distinctive of their particular historical influences, they are all derived from the same major principles. Initially all use a form of practice which links the quiescence of "stance keeping" (*zhanzhuang*) with various media of dynamic transition. The term "zhuang ba" is sometimes used to convey this principle. The practical components of zhuang ba are often utilized through the practice of xingyi's splitting fist (*pi quan*) and/or the half-step (*ban bu*).

  Equally important is to eliminate excessive enthusiasm or emotion during practice. Emotions cloud the awareness to subtle internal sensations. Normally we are accustomed to fueling the structure through emotional release or willpower. Xingyi seeks to eliminate dependence on will-derived power.

61

- **What is the function of zhuang ba?**

"Stance keeping" or "standing" provides a basis by which transitional movements may originate from a point or a center. In this way there is no wavering in either form or awareness while one shifts from stillness to motion.

Zhuang ba should be practiced until it feels smooth and comfortable. Its practice assists in regulating and normalizing the qi and blood flow of the body. Varying body types have predilections towards particular strengths and weaknesses. Thus, zhuang ba may help one overcome individual deficiencies which are liable to hinder one's development during later training stages.

- **What about xingyi's martial considerations?**

In the beginning stages of xingyi training, detailed martial applications should not be overly stressed. It is more important to emphasize correct form.

Left: swallow posture. Right: monkey posture.

- **So a student should first concentrate on developing structure and mind?**

Even though the rudimentary concepts of xingyi are devised to develop a strong link between body and mind, one should not initially become overwhelmed in this aspect of the training. At the beginning, it is sufficient enough to train with one idea in mind: "One part moves, all parts move." Focus on how to begin and how to end a particular movement. Details like whether the hand or the foot or the hips should move first needn't be overly emphasized. In addition, specific angles and minute postural concerns should not be overly focused upon. Once the body begins to respond naturally, the specifics of movement may then be given progressive attention.

As in the elementary stages of any type of physical training, students may initially have difficulty controlling their bodies to the degree they desire. One of xingyi's primary undertakings is to train the body so that it may behave as the mind wishes. In theory, when the yi (mind) moves the entire body moves. In this way, the fusion of xing (form) and yi (mind) may begin.

Left: monkey posture. Right: taixing posture.

• **What do you feel is xingyi's primary guide for practice?**

Practice until the body is balanced. Regulation of the central energy channels in the body, especially the conception vessel (*ren mai*) and the governing channel (*du mai*), should be stressed. Conceptually, xingyi seeks to create a wave that runs up and down the spinal column. Some people refer to this phenomenon as the Microcosmic Orbit (*xiao zhou tian*). Comprehension of body mechanics should also accompany this spinal wave?

• **What is the meaning of internal and external?**

This dichotomy is not really accurate in differentiating the various branches of martial arts. It does, however, differentiate the *yi* (mind) aspect of training within that dichotomy. Hence, the internal arts stress yi to a greater degree than the external arts. This is not to say that the external arts do not include yi training. Practices like standing (*zhanzhuang*), qi gong, and meditation are also included in the external arts. The difference lies in degree and direction of emphasis. The internal arts stress yi training as the basis of their initial training practices whereas the external arts tend to begin with body conditioning first and turn to yi development later. Principally both internal and external traditions adhere to the practice of combining the interior and the exterior as one (*nei wai he jing*).

• **What are the major differences between the three internal martial arts of taijiquan, xingyiquan, and baquaquan?**

In principle, taiji, xingyi and bagua are closely related. Again, their differences can best be discerned in regard to degree of emphasis. For instance, taiji is often noted for its aptness in regard to adhering and attaching skills. It develops refined skill in detecting shifts of emptiness and fullness. Its power is mainly issued at the waist. Taiji attracts with emptiness and then concludes with hardness.

Bagua's emphasis on changing angles in order to maintain a superior vantage point is well developed. Its power is mainly derived by way of the foot. It initiates with hardness and concludes with softness. Xingyi's power is most obviously apparent in its forward and backward transitions. Its striking and attacking motions are designed to destroy one's root. Its power is mainly expressed through the hand. Xingyi enters with hardness and concludes with softness.

- **Are there any aspects of internal development you feel are normally misrepresented?**

Many teachers mistakenly suggest to their students that internal martial art techniques must not be practiced with strength. In reality, a student should be advised not to employ excessive strength. Use of excessive strength may divert one's focus away from the yi aspect of internal cultivation.

Swallow postures.

- **What is *fajing* (issuing power) training in xingyi?**

It is quite difficult to talk about fajing unless one specifies the conditions under which fajing is employed. The variety of situations are numerous with regard to what fajing expresses; therefore, the applications are also numerous. Furthermore, because fajing does not occur in a vacuum, it requires the correct positioning or circumstances with respect to one's objective. To apply fajing into a perfectly stable opponent will not produce a positive outcome. Fajing doesn't always imply a positive outcome. Fajing is usefully applied once an imbalance is noted; hence, one can use fajing with the spine, hand, elbow, shoulder, etc., or with a half-step.

- **What does the *jing* in *fajing* refer to?**

Jing refers to the synergistic effect produced as a result of combining xing and yi. Traditionally, this means that power is released from one point or is concentrated at one point. The mind concentrates physical strength at one point and then suddenly issues from that point. This requires timing, control, and a support point. Correct structural alignment and smooth forward and backward mobility provide a basis for the actualization of this power.

- **Does yi training enlist the help of any outside training apparatus?**

Of course, for example, emphasis upon training the yi (intent) may proceed by using minimal striking motion while hitting a sand bag. Let your yi penetrate deeply into the bag. In this way, reaction upon impact may also be researched.

- **What is *xingyi neigong?***

In essence, neigong is the term used to refer to endeavors such as meditation, qigong, and various longlife exercises. In the Chinese medical sense, neigong is an order of practice involving the regulation of qi and blood and thus deals with imbalance in the body. The neigong practiced in xingyi may differ in accordance to the particular style in question, whereas neigong practice may be carried out while assuming various body positions (sitting, standing, laying). In the martial arts, however, it is *zhanzhuang* (standing keeping) that is most often practiced.

- **What is the purpose of *zhanzhuang?***

Zhanzhuang practice can be used to change one's manner of applying fajing. By resting the mind (central nervous system) and consequently ridding the mind of anxiety, zhanzhuang instills relaxation while applying fajing and thus conserves energy. In this way, one does not rely on willpower-induced strength and hence avoids overstimulating the nervous system.

Additionally, zhanzhuang establishes several internal and external alignments that help to correct imbalances in the body's alignment and which assist in maintaining a feeling of being centered. These alignments stabilize the *xin* (heart mind) and regulate the qi, allowing for a point of awareness to originate from a center. The chest should be hollowed, the back and shoulders rounded and the elbows sunk. The heart should be open and relaxed, accompanied by the feeling that the body doesn't exist. This can be accomplished by imagining oneself as an enormous Buddha gazing out over a great expanse (such as the horizon or the ocean) while standing. A sense of vastness and a feeling of one-pointed awareness may develop.

Standing posture (*zhanzhuang*).

A similar notion is expressed in "be like a mountain," which refers to sensations of both expansion and stillness. Cultivation of stillness sensitizes one's awareness to subtle internal movement. In this state one's internal body rhythms may be realized. The breath will then regulate itself in natural coordination with those rhythms. Ultimately one wishes to coordinate one's own body rhythm with the larger universal rhythms. This level of awareness leads to expansion of the yi and thus greater command over it.

Left: monkey application. Right: pi quan application.

• **During standing practice, what should one do if pain is experienced?**
This indicates there may be pre-existing blood and qi disharmonies, perhaps due to previous injury or disease in the body. Practice of this nature may temporarily renew past disharmonies until the body is able to restabilize itself. Because zhanzhuang seeks relaxation, pain is indicative of areas that have not yet relaxed, but, as relaxation progresses, pain will gradually abate.

• **Should the body be totally relaxed?**
Well, relaxation doesn't imply total limpness. It suggests relaxation within limits. This allows ease in applying fajing, awareness of each part of the body, and hence greater sensitivity to internal body rhythms.
Developing body sensitivity teaches one to combine physical strength and the mind. Accordingly, when the mind desires the body to act, the body may do so with natural ease. In effect there is conservation of energy instead of loss. This is a consummate requirement in developing fajing without depleting the body's resources.

• **Should the breath be concentrated at the *dantian*?***
The problem of sinking the yi to the dantian is actually a matter of controlling the mind. The dantian is not only representative of the lower abdominal region but is also representative of other areas of the body often including the body as a whole. Initially however, one should lead the yi to the lower abdominal one.

Dantian ("cinnabar field") refers to an area in the lower part of the abdomen located about three inches below the navel.

- **How many hours a day should one practice?**

When qigong practice exceeds one's physical and mental limits it becomes a practice of will. At that point, as fatigue increases, internal sensitivity diminishes. Therefore, one should avoid practice sessions which follow predesignated time frames. This defeats the purpose. Rather, begin with the notion of "one minute of practice produces one minute of result." The idea is to give all one can during practice, without surpassing one's current limitations. In this way, one may assist the body in healing any blood and qi disharmonies, instead of depleting their resources.

FIVE ELEMENTS

pi quan – splitting fist
zhuan quan – drilling fist
pao quan – pounding fist
beng quan – crushing fist
heng quan – crossing fist

- **What is the practice of *wuxing* (five elements/fists) for?**

Each of the fists manifest fajing in a different manner: pi quan's power travels in an upward to downward configuration; zhuan quan, downward to upward; beng quan, backward and forward; pao quan, from inside to outside; and heng quan, from outside to inside. Wu xing isolates energy configurations by practicing one movement over and over again. The yi and the physical movement are trained to become very tightly connected. Ultimately, xingyi seeks to integrate the five fists into a single energy unit. In this way, change from one fist to another may proceed without interruption and without anticipation.

- **Isn't this also the function of xingyi's linking form?**

Yes. The practice of *lian huan* (linking form) and *xiang shen* (mutual creation form) assist in further expanding the yi. Thus, one's presence of mind may progressively develop. This practice manifests as a skill which is sometimes referred to as *jin cou*. This term is indicative of the way in which one movement smoothly blends with a preceding movement. So, in effect, there is no physical or mental break from one motion to the next. A bond between the xing and the yi is developed.

"*Sheng sheng bu xi*" is an axiom which is suggestive of endless succession and/or instantaneous creation. Hence, it is indicative of the seamless continuity which develops as individual movements are linked together through linking form practice.

Martially speaking, the objective is to make your yi more expansive than your opponent's. Xingyi's linking form is effective in this respect. If one inspects the linking form, it will be noticed that beng quan (crushing fist) is relied on a great deal as one of the main connective movements. The simplicity of beng quan allows smooth integration of both form and consciousness.

67

- **What does "twelve animal" training emphasize?**

It should first be understood that xingyi's arsenal essentially consists of only five forms. However, there are various expressions of technique for each one of the five. The twelve animals are made up of those same five original components. For instance, horse is like the inverse of zhuan quan. Dragon is like double pi quan; Chicken is like pao quan; taixing (a mythical bird) is like heng quan, etc. Each animal is simply a variation of one of the five original forms, the difference being, aside from just variation of the physical configurations, the addition of spirit.

Left: beng quan application. Right: heng quan application.

- **How does one define spirit from the xingyi point of view?**

Spirit is connotative of characteristic and ability. In order for an animal to flourish in nature it must have a specialty. An animal's spirit accounts for its ability to adapt. For instance, the monkey is nimble, yet cautious. Its craftiness is displayed by its hit-and-run tactics. The determination of the bear in combination with its tremendous strength is powerful enough to uproot a tree. The ripping and tearing of the fighting chicken's beak and claws characterize its ruthless spirit when protecting its young. The tiger is quite fierce and has the ability to use its mass to pounce upon its prey. As for the dragon, it exhibits rising and falling motions; its springing movement demonstrates the use of the spinal wave. It is a very powerful creature. It fears nothing. It has no limitations. It may wander about in either heaven or hell.

The infusion of form with spirit creates a considerable range of possibility within the xingyi system. It allows for movements to change inside of movements or for change to occur within change. For instance, if xingyi's pi quan adopts the spirit of dragon, pi quan will appear with a greater amplitude of the spinal wave. In such an instance, pi quan may acquire an obviously expanded springing quality to its motion. The basis of the form remains the same, but there are obvious transformations in the flavor of the overall motion.

On the other hand, if pi quan adopts the crafty and cautious spirit of the monkey, the spinal wave will appear quick and relatively compact. The circumstances at hand should determine the spiritual expression of the form. For instance, the monkey must consider its natural weaknesses and strengths in light of the opponents it encounters. If attacked by a much larger foe, the monkey may have to rely on its cunning nature in order to equalize its inherent deficiencies. Like a hunter, one must choose the appropriate weapon for each situation.

- **If form may be altered in accordance to spirit, then I would assume the opposite is also true?**

That's right! Let's use pi quan again to investigate this problem. Pi quan may be delivered as a palm strike to the top of the head, but that same motion may be changed to piercing strikes to the eyes. In this case, the spirit is the same but the form changes. Or take beng quan for example. It can be applied in a Shaolin boxing-like fashion or in a manner suggestive of taijiquan, but it is still beng quan. What has changed is the mind.

Wu xing's five constructs may change depending on the mood of the practitioner. Big may change to small, or small to big.

- **What is the meaning of the half-step (banbu) and the consecutive step (jinbu)?**

Moving the body from point to point without losing proper body alignment can be carried out in the most expedient fashion by employing the half-step. The half-step may move either forward or backward. The full-step is simply two successive half-steps.

Zuan quan application.

- **Can you give an example of their martial application?**

Sure. From a stationary position the body is able to roll back with a half-step and blend with an opponent's rhythm and then proceed back at him with a half-step as the circle returns. An additional half-step (consecutive step) may be included just as the opponent's root is broken in order to accelerate his imbalance.

With a half-step, the body's posture remains balanced throughout. Therefore, one's reactions are swift and one's power does not diminish. The consecutive step allows one to transfer one's weight with proper body alignment (*zhen jing*) into a more advantageous position to employ fajing. Fajing may also be amplified when it coordinates with movement of the body through space. When one becomes relatively proficient in moving forward and backward with the half-step, he should begin to practice angular half-stepping.

- **How should one control a fighting situation with xingyi?**

One should restrain from greedy attacks. Eat at your opponents defenses a little at a time. When striking, don't over-extend. Xingyi always keeps a little reach in reserve. If each time only seventy percent of the reach is used, then each successive movement may be delivered with relative ease. Don't try to end things with one over-extended motion.

Furthermore, one's yi should not break as the body moves through a distance of from three to six meters. Practice with an appropriate mental focus helps develop uninterrupted mobility.

One of xingyi's major objectives is to control forward and backward body movement. Forward and backward motion should be established in combination with both fighting technique and the ability to fajing. Many martial styles are designed to deliver power from a stationary position but may momentarily lose their structural alignment while changing postures; hence, they may also be temporarily unable to issue power within that transitional period. So, in effect, their range of motion is actually quite small. One of xingyi's prominent features is its large range of motion. Essentially, larger range of motion is indicative of one's ability to issue power from not only a stationary position but also while on the move.

- **What about the technical aspects of fighting?**

When fighting, first dodge the attack and then move forward towards the opponent. The three points (*san jian*, which represents the center-line created by alignment of the nose, hands and feet) should be guarded as this type of movement is carried out. Xingyi advises that the fist remain over one's center-line so that minimal lateral movement may ward off an oncoming attack.

Moreover, your yi should be superior to your opponent's. The fastest thing between two points is intent (*yi*). While facing an opponent, you must first catch his mind and then catch his body tempo. Catching the mind requires that there are fewer breaks in your awareness than your opponent's, thereby allowing you to seize the right moment to attack. Thus, merging with your opponent's motion (tempo) requires your yi to also merge with his yi. When you can smoothly catch your opponent's tempo, then you will have no problem in maintaining control. This is *xin fa* (heart/mind method).*

* Xin fa is knowledge that is based on experience, and hence uncovers the heart or essence of that which is in question.

- **What problems do most people have with their xingyi stances?**

The biggest problem most people have is letting their hips arch up (sticking the buttocks out). This is often due to soreness of the back leg experienced during the practice of stance keeping. If the hips arch out of alignment, then the back leg will be unable to adequately move into a closed stance. Consequently, if the back leg turns out too much, a resulting unstable posture makes it impossible to execute fajing.

On the other hand, the stance may be too closed. This means that everything is being pulled inward too much, which in turn creates an imbalance and an unstable structure.

Problems may also result from using too much strength while standing. This causes muscular tension, which in turn impedes the relaxation necessary for awareness of internal movement. Continuous practice of this nature overdevelops willpower.

Another common difficulty is poor integration of body movements. For instance, as in common pi quan, the front hand moves but the back hand does not move in coordination with it. Or the movement of the hands and feet are not synchronized. Essentially, xingyi's movements are not extremely complicated, but the quality of their execution should be of a high standard.

Mr. Luo Dexiu with students Marcus Brinkman (l.) and Dietmar Stubenbuam (r.).

- What are your personal thoughts about how to apply the five elements in a fighting situation?

Actually, technique is a matter of individual expression. So, select one of the forms that you favor and adapt it to fit every kind of encounter. One may execute continual attacks with one particular fist while keeping in mind that the attack is only to initiate an initial response or a defensive action from your opponent. This reasoning is in line with the idea of first securing a support point and a more advantageous position from which to proceed. After a response, attack again with the same kind of fist. This type of practice should be done with the help of a training partner so that your knowledge of application may be first intimately linked with the subconscious.

Start by using simple attacks. Practice all manner of bridging (low, high, left, right, etc.). Occasionally, let your opponent attack while trying your best to employ a specific fist as a defensive maneuver. Train forward and backward movement on both sides and proceed with the idea of changing your movements from big to small and from small to big.

- Do you have any final comments?

As one practices xingyi, if there are areas of deficiency, one should not borrow from other systems in order to make up for any gaps of knowledge.

chapter 6

American Boxing and Chinese Xingyi
~A Comparison

by Robert Lin-yi Yu, M.A.

Left: Robert Yu. Right: In Taipei with his xingyi teacher, Hong Yixiang.
All photos courtesy of Robert Yu.

Introduction

When I first studied with Master Hong Yixiang in Taipei, Taiwan, in September 1969, it was an opportune time to learn from him. He was a young master at 47 years old and active in demonstrating forms and doing light sparring. He hit with such power that you felt blessed not to go full contact with him. On rare occasions, he would spar with senior students who put on two thick, Chinese-style chest protectors to protect themselves from Hong's blows. During this time, and into the early 1970's, Hong was surrounded by eager young senior students who were beginning to establish themselves as premier fighters in "open-style" national tournaments. By the mid-1970's, Hong became known for the training of boxers using the xingyi style, a soft-internal system of Chinese martial arts, and winning all weight divisions his school entered.

It was my good fortune to be with Master Hong during the height of his teaching. Growing up in Minnesota, I played football for Hamline University, in St. Paul as a starting linebacker/guard (1964-66). So I was in decent shape and accustomed to the rigors of training. I was introduced to Master Hong by Dan Hickey, a U.S. Marine who was with Hong for five years. Hong had evening classes for 3 to 4 hours, six days a week. In addition, during my last six months, I had morning classes with Master Hong and trained privately with him every day from eight until noon.

In June 1971, I wrote an article about Hong for *Echo* magazine, an English-language magazine published in Taiwan. Upon returning to America in the fall of 1972, I was fascinated by Robert W. Smith's books on Chinese martial arts and his earlier encounter with Master Hong. Reading them, I felt I was reliving my time in Taiwan. I remembered Hong's oldest son, Ah Ju, asking me if I knew of a Mr. Smith from America. The Hong family had fond memories of Mr. Smith.

Before we proceed further, two points needs to be made. First, perhaps there will be some Sinophiles who are uncomfortable with the comparison of the art of xingyi to what they view as the brutal sport of Western-style boxing. To them I must point out that Hong demanded practical usefulness in his art. I think Hong's major contribution was to put the "punch" back into the soft-internal system by rejuvenating and testing the xingyi system in fighting matches.

Second, the xingyi system is based on self-defense, so that kicks, grappling, and joint locking (*qinna*) are within the scope of its fighting techniques. However, during the intense boxing practices in Hong's gym, during months of full-contact sparring, and during all the "open-style" national tournaments that Hong's boys were victorious, the fist or the open palm was the main weapon used in actual fighting. This article will focus on xingyi's contribution to practical boxing applications.

An Eastern and a Western Approach

In the modern world, Western boxing, particularly the American style, is the most popular example of fist fighting we have today. Professional matches attract worldwide attention, Olympic boxing involves most nations, and amateur bouts and Golden Glove bouts stir up local interest. Because the popularity of Western style boxing is widespread, its rules and regulations are known to all fans and its techniques and training regimen are celebrated by boxing aficionados everywhere. However, the ancient system of Chinese boxing is little known in the West.

Eastern forms of martial arts have been stereotyped and often are perceived only as karate or taekwondo forms. In fact, karate and taekwondo have so dominated the landscape of the American perception of Asian martial arts that the Chinese martial arts systems and theories are often overlooked.

One of the older boxing systems widely practiced in China is xingyi. Its tradition goes back hundreds of years, although written history traces its lineage to the early 1800's. Its training will not dazzle you with high leaps or spinning kicks. There is nothing fancy about it. Yet its purpose is clear. Of the Chinese systems, xingyi stands out as essentially a puncher's art.

It is interesting to compare Western boxing with xingyi. Their similarities give credence to the basic universality of the art of boxing, while their differences enrich our knowledge of boxing techniques. A study of the Chinese boxing system gives us insight into an older Asian interpretation of the art of fist fighting.

Xingyi embodies the ideals of a soft-internal martial system. It comes from the same soft, internal family as taijiquan and bagua. Spiritually, it focuses on the flow of *qi* (life force energy), as a meditation in motion, and on holding postures. Physically, it

74

works on the pelvic area (*gua*) as the center of action. It uses relaxed movements to train grounding and rooting and to increase the flexibility of the waist and legs.

Both the American boxing system and xingyi divide their attention between training the hands and the feet. Above the waist, the American system emphasizes specific hand techniques and hand speed. Below the waist, the American system trains foot movement in conjunction with hand movement and talks of using the hips when throwing power punches.

Xingyi views the legs and arms in terms of coiling circles and springs. The Chinese boxer is trained to initiate power and movement from the pelvic area (*gua*).

A comparison of American and Chinese boxing techniques can give us some interesting insights into the art of boxing.

Boxing Stances

The main features of the American style "on guard" stance are as follows:
1) If the boxer is right-handed, his or her "on-guard" stance will lead with the left leg; that is, the left leg is in front of the right and it is reversed if the boxer is left-handed.
2) The feet are approximately parallel to each other and spread apart with the left foot forward. The left foot is placed in front of the right foot for a right-handed fighter. This is reversed for a left-handed fighter. Again, for a right-handed fighter, the lead foot is the left foot. The right hand is held back as a power punch, known in boxing terms as a "straight right."
3) The weight is evenly distributed between both feet—a 50/50 stance—although there is often slightly more weight on the front foot.
4) The chin is held close to the left shoulder and lowered an inch or two. The left shoulder can be lifted an inch or two to further protect the chin.
5) The heel of the right foot is kept off the floor.
6) Both elbows are held inward to protect the ribs.
7) Both knees are slightly flexed.
8) The entire body is relaxed.

In contrast, the main points of the xingyi "on-guard" stance are:
1) If the boxer is right-handed, he or she will lead with the right leg and right hand, and the reverse if he or she is left-handed.
2) The boxer stands more squarely to the opponent, and the right-handed boxer's left foot is behind and at a 45-degree angle to the right foot. Xingyi boxers lead with their most powerful side. Thus, if one is right-handed, one would lead with the right hand and right foot.
3) The xingyi boxer trains in a 90/10 stance. That is, roughly, 90 percent of the weight is on the back foot, with 10 percent of the weight on the front foot.
4) The head is held upright, the chin is held down towards the chest, and the back is aligned.

75

5) Both feet are kept flat on the floor.

6) Both hands are extended from the chest with arms neither straight nor bent, but curved. Both elbows are pointed downward.

7) Both knees are slightly flexed.

8) The entire body is relaxed.

Comment on Stances

The Chinese boxer is taught to lead with the power side of the body. Therefore, in American boxing parlance, the Chinese boxers train the "jab" to be a devastating knock-down first punch (not unlike Mohammed Ali's left jab; perhaps Ali's left-side was his power side?). Xingyi training techniques help develop a relaxed waist area, while grounding and rooting the feet.

"Gua" has been translated to mean the "waist" in English; however, in xingyi, the term means the region where the lower torso meets the legs. It is this area that involves the pelvic girdle and hip joints. But more to the point, "gua" describes action. The gua involves the movement of this pelvic area; the hip joints; and the muscles, tendons, and ligaments that are engaged in this area when force is compressed downward or released upward. Xingyi exercises train the body to move this powerful area that connects the spine to the legs to be like a spring: coiling and uncoiling. Xingyi "trains" the gua and makes the boxer conscious of the gua as a source of power and movement. Xingyi boxers learn to relax and develop flexibility in the gua with range of motion exercises. Ultimately, this area will be used to generate power in the fists.

Chinese boxers are taught to extend their arms, not straight or bent, but curved away from the body as a defense, whereas American boxers are taught to hold their elbows close to their ribs to protect them.

During an actual fight, both the Western-style boxer and the xingyi boxer can come off their heels and box on their toes. However, during training in the xingyi forms, the Chinese boxer is required to keep both feet flat on the floor, this is done to exercise the lower legs, the ankles, and shins, to increase their flexibility. Moreover, maintaining the 90/10 stance teaches the xingyi boxer to practice punching angles with the maximum leverage below the waist to enhance power through rooting and grounding.

"To ground" and "to root" are closely related concepts that point to the importance of the feet and earth as the source of power. "To ground" means to be steadfast, to be firm and solid, to anchor and hold the position. The concept of rooting has similar connotations but includes absorbing so as to draw up energy from the earth or ground. The power of a punch is measured by this ability to ground and to root. The development of grounding/rooting is a major part of xingyi exercises. Chinese boxers habitually wiggle and squeeze their toes and even cup their feet to strengthen this feeling of grounding/rooting. Furthermore, through training, the duality of the yin-yang takes place and xingyi boxers begin to realize that grounding/rooting is enhanced by relaxation and that this ability to relax allows them to react and adjust quickly to change. The feeling of gripping the ground and relaxing is one of the keys to developing power and speed.

Both American and xingyi boxing stress proper standing stances. It is important to emphasize that the xingyi boxing stance is very similar to the American stance and unlike some wide karate stances. Hong Yixiang, one of the most renowned martial artists in Taiwan who taught xingyi, was well aware of the tradeoff between a wide stance and mobility. The American and Chinese boxing systems share the rationale for proper distance in the boxing stance. Both American- and Chinese-style boxers have discovered that having too wide a stance reduces mobility, while having a narrow stance reduces ground/root and thereby lessens the power in the punch. Xingyi has never been simplified to the point of Japanese and Korean systems, which have often evolved to emphasize kicking techniques over hand techniques. Hong frequently admonished, "Good hands will defeat feet." What he meant by this was that outboxing your opponent would take away the effectiveness of his kicks.

Another important difference in the two boxing styles is that xingyi boxers are taught to square their waist toward the opponent. While American stylists would argue that this exposes the boxer more, the Chinese stylists are trained to use the gua rather than the hips, to generate power. Chinese boxers believe that power comes from the lower torso, pelvic area, and the area of the breathing center (*dantian*). When punching, the Chinese boxer trains to lift the gua to use the deep muscles in the pelvic area for power, and not to rely solely on the horizontal rotation of the hips to generate power, which leads to a rigid back leg position.

Punching Techniques

A clear description of the orthodox American-style boxing style was given to me during discussions with Mr. Bob Lynch. A gentleman and former professional boxer, he is a long-time boxing trainer and coach at the University of Wisconsin. Lynch lists the five basic hand techniques from the standard right-handed "on-guard" stance as:

1) the jab thrown by the left hand
2) three basic right-hand punches:
   a. the straight right, a power punch, and two counter-punches
   b. the overhand right, and
   c. the right cross
3) the hook thrown by the left hand; and an uppercut thrown by either hand
4) the right uppercut, and
5) the left uppercut.

When an American-style boxer throws a power punch, he is taught to twist or rotate the hips to allow his entire body to be involved in the punch rather than punching with just his arms and shoulders. In throwing the two basic punches, the jab and the straight right, the rear leg must be, if not completely straight, at least rigid as the fist makes contact. The rear ankle too, must be rigid and extended somewhat. The rear heel comes up off the floor and the boxer pushes off the ball of the foot. It is said that a powerful punch is thrown when the boxer is able to punch from the feet to the top of the head, involving the entire body in the punch. In addition, the punching arm or the wrist must have a snapping action to it. The blow must be delivered with great force and speed.

American boxers practice speed in their punching skills. The speed bag and punching bag are used to develop speed when throwing punches. In Chinese boxing, Hong emphasized that a fist can come from any direction and at all angles: "A fist comes from a circle; it can come anywhere—360 degrees." So, in xingyi there is no distinction made between types of punches. A punch simply is called a "punch," and it can be thrown by either the left hand or right hand. It can come from any direction: up, down, or sideways.

When punching, the Chinese boxer is taught to internally pull the gua to generate power from the feet through grounding/rooting into the legs. This is referred to as "concealed energy." Visually, the rear foot can be pulled forward in this action, and appears as a stutter step (*banbu*). When advancing forward and punching, the xingyi boxer makes this action even clearer by pulling the gua with each punch. Simultaneously, short and choppy steps will follow the forward movement.

An important difference between the two boxing styles is that, rather than lifting the heel of the rear foot and stiffening when throwing a straight punch as in the American style, the Chinese boxer is taught to sink or visualize drilling downward while punching, thereby maximizing grounding/rooting for power. Importantly, this movement requires the training necessary for the development of flexibility in the pelvic area and lower legs to accomplish this action.

Comment on Punching Technique

Chinese boxers are taught to view a punch as coming from a 360-degree circle. A punch can come from any angle: up, down, or sideways. By the same token, a punch can be thrown from any angle, and, for the most part, is left to spontaneous instinct whereas American stylists give much more emphasis to the types of punches. Western-style purists make distinctions between a right cross and a straight right and have been known to argue that one cannot throw a "hook" with the right hand in a left-lead stance.

Both American and Chinese boxers are taught to punch using not just the arms and shoulders, but the entire body. The difference is in how the boxers are trained to generate power. The American boxers focus on the "hips" and are taught to rotate them when punching. This is a twisting motion and results in a stiff rear leg used to generate power from the rear leg upward. The Chinese boxers focus on the "gua," not the hips, and are taught to use the deep muscles, tendons, and ligaments that surround the entire pelvis. This focuses on the use of the pelvic area in tandem with exercises that increase lower leg flexibility so that the dynamics of movement is likened to a spring or coiling motion, with the rear leg flexing rather than stiffening when throwing a punch.

Western-style boxing's often repeated phrase, "He has fast hands" or "He has quick hands" is a different idea of power. Hong used to say that "speed is just fast," and has less to do with the force behind the blow than grounding/rooting. To Hong's way of thinking, training hand speed as a boxing skill was overrated. In fact, he dismissed Western-style boxing's emphasis on hand speed saying: "One only needs to go as fast as one's opponent." Hong pointed out that simple relaxation of the shoulders and arms increases hand speed. So, instead of concerning himself with hand speed, Hong concentrated on techniques described below that developed power in the punch.

FOOTWORK: FORWARD, BACKWARD, AND SIDEWAYS

American Style

When the boxer moves forward (in the left foot lead stance), he moves his left foot first, and follows with his right. When he moves backward, he first steps back with the right foot, and then follows with his left or lead foot. To move left, the boxer steps sideways with his left foot and follows with his right. When he moves right, he steps to his right with his right foot and follows with his left.

Chinese Style

When the boxer moves forward (in the right foot lead stance), he shifts weight onto and pushes off with his left foot. He then plants his right foot and pulls from the gua to move his left foot forward. When the boxer moves backward, he shifts weight onto his right foot and pushes off and plants his left foot, and then pulls from the gua to move his right foot back. When the boxer moves to the left, he steps perpendicular to his opponent with his left foot and pulls his right foot forward from the gua. When the boxer moves to the right, he steps to the outside of his opponent with his right foot and pulls his left foot forward from the gua.

Comment on Footwork

In American-style boxing, when the boxer moves forward, no emphasis is given to the rear leg, and when moving backward, no emphasis is given to the front leg. The boxer simply is trained to slide the leg. However, despite this lack of attention to the movement of the leg, American boxing trainers will remind you that boxing footwork is nothing like ballroom dancing.

In xingyi-style boxing, the boxer moves forward by stepping forward with the right leg, but is trained to move the left leg with a quick tuck of the pelvis or, as xingyi instructor Frank Juszczyk (New Mexico) says, with a "hitch" motion of the gua. This is one of the keys to the Chinese boxing technique. First, by using the gua to pull up the leg, the boxer moves and simultaneously establishes grounding/rooting. By maintaining this balance, the xingyi boxer is able to punch with power. Again, when moving backwards, the boxer's forward leg is moved back by the pull of the gua, again enabling the fighter to instantly regain grounding/rooting. Second, the pelvis is anatomically the body's center of gravity and, by the xingyi movement method, it is the center of action. Such logic underlies the naturalness of the xingyi style. Xingyi technique uses pelvic motion to move the leg. This allows the body to move in a integrated way so that the arms and legs respond to block and punch with power and speed.

Finally, xingyi boxers are taught to "train" the gua. They are also taught to "train" relaxation. Varying the speed when doing practice routines is one method used to encourage relaxed movement. Hong noted, "Slow is harder to do than fast." A relaxed gua allows the grounding/rooting of the feet to reach the fists. Relaxed legs allow the grounding/rooting of the feet to rise up to the arms. Relaxed arms and shoulders allow the power from the gua to emerge from the fists.

The best description of the application of the soft-internal system is from the *Taijiquan Classics*: "The motion should be rooted in the feet, released through the legs, controlled by the waist (*gua*), and manifested through the fingers." Xingyi boxers read the word "fingers" in the above quote as "fists." While Hong may have felt taijiquan's "push hands" was a valuable training exercise, he had little patience with soft-internal system practitioners who talked about the their system's superiority but were unable to defend themselves in a actual fight.

HEAD POSITION

American Style
The boxer's head is not in a straight, upright position. Proper chin placement should be head down with the chin close to the chest. Furthermore, the boxer may lift his left shoulder an inch or two to further protect his chin.

Xingyi Style
The boxer's head should be erect, with the occipital bone ("jade pillow"), gently lifting upwards. The coccyx should be gently tilted forward to ensure correct alignment of the entire spine.

Comment on Head Position
The chin-down position in American boxing is used to minimize the head as a target. In xingyi boxing, the head and the spine are aligned to ensure the proper flow of energy. The position of the back is crucial for balance and centering and thereby generating power and the flow of vital energy (*qi*). The importance of spinal alignment allows the flow of vital energy to come together with intentional force, or muscular force (*li*), so that maximum force (*jing*) is created.

• • •

This comparison of the American and Chinese boxing systems offers a global view on the art of boxing. In the earlier influx of martial arts from Japan and Korea to America, the Chinese systems have been largely hidden from view. A spotlight on xingyi reveals lessons on boxing techniques that are valuable to all practitioners of the "sweet science" of boxing.

TECHNICAL SECTION

A) The Hook

Here is a good depiction of Western style boxing's use of the hips and the raising of the back heel when punching (A3-5). Xingyi trains the same punch by sinking downward (A1-2).

B) The Straight Left

In the Chinese xingyi style, a right-handed person is trained to "lead" with the right foot, thereby throwing a right jab and a left straight punch (B1-2). It is opposite for the Western trained boxers (B3-4).

C) The Jab

In xingyi training, it is common to use the "right lead" for a right-handed person. Thus, the right jab is often the lead punch (C1-2). In contrast, Western style boxers train using a left jab for a right-handed person while using a "left lead" stance (C3-4).

D) The Uppercut

In Western-style punching, the back heel rises from twisting the hips (D3-4). A difference in xingyi is that the gua moves and springs off the rear ankle (D1-2).

Acknowledgments

The author would like to especially thank Bob Lynch for his generous help on Western boxing techniques. Thanks to Dr. Victor Yu and Joyce Yu, Dr. Frank Juszczyk, and Dr. Peter Wolff; and students Bill Karls, Ton Karls, Paula Robbins, Games Gonzales, Dale and Cathy Ivarie, Niki McGlathery, Nile Ostenso, Alec Stanley, and Lynette Penewell for their assistance.

chapter 7

Hong Yixiang & Five Fists
Xingyi Boxing in Old Taipei

by Robert Yu, M.A.

Left: Hong Yixiang's painting of Bodhidharma and the twelve animals of xingyi, which hung in his office. Right: Hong at a banquet in Taipei, 1971. *All illustrations courtesy of Robert Yu.*

Over three decades ago, I studied xingyiquan ("form-mind boxing") from Master Hong Yixiang in Taipei, Taiwan. When he passed away in June, 1993, the then President of Taiwan, Lee Tunghui, mourned the passing of one of China's living treasures. Master Hong has since become a well-known teacher because so many of his students have carried on his teaching and have spread his influence throughout Asia, Europe, and the United States.

I began training with Hong in September, 1969, and stayed with him for two and a half years. He taught classes six days a week, for three hours each evening. I never missed a class. His evening classes were held in the gymnasium of an old elementary school. The gymnasium was a large open space with an uneven, cracked concrete floor. The windows around the gym were without panes, broken out long ago. I never noticed these windows until the winter months when it got cold outside and the doors were pulled shut. On the front wall hung two large Chinese characters symbolizing "loyalty" and "respect."

This neighborhood was the oldest section of Taipei, the Yen Ping District. The buildings were simple and elegant three-storied red-brick apartment houses that shared shaded porticos out onto the street. They were homes to generations of families living together. Hong's home was here, on the same block as his office and the gym where we practiced. When I returned to Taiwan fifteen years later, much of the old neighborhood remained intact; however, the old gym had been torn down.

1) Two of Hong's top students (Lao Lei and Lo Ca) enjoying tea in his office. Notice the hallway lined with training gear, where Robert Yu trained with him in the mornings; and the student chart with pictures and names of past and present students.

2) Robert Yu's "student card." On the back there is a monthly chart which gives spaces for it to be used for four years. Hong would apply his signature chop for each month of attendance.

3) Hong at his office with shelves of bottled herbs.

4) Tricia Yu standing under the shaded portico in front of Hong's office in Taipei, 1971.

Hong would usually stroll in shortly after class began. He wore dark baggy pants, a gray, long-sleeved T-shirt and tennis shoes. He would be smoking an unfiltered cigarette of "Long Life" brand name. After classes the students would often go to a nearby tea house and talk into the night. Occasionally, Hong would join us.

During my last six months in Taiwan, I sought additional training with Hong. I trained for four hours in the mornings at his office. His office smelled of the herbs he used in his practice of Chinese medicine. He had rows of drawers and shelves of brown glass bottles filled with herbs. On one wall there was a picture painted by Hong of Bodhidharma surrounded by twelve animals that inspired particular xingyi forms. On the high office walls were hung impressive ebony plaques with Chinese characters in gold leaf.

On the other side of Hong's office there was a long, narrow hallway. I would do the classic "five elements" (*wuxing*) form up and down this hallway, from the front of his office to the back room where there was a small kitchen where morning and afternoon teas were made. In this hallway, thick Chinese-style chest protectors, head gear, and light-weight Chinese-style boxing gloves were hung on hooks to dry out as best as they could in this hot, humid climate. Further down the hallway, there was a wooden chart with the names of past and present students inked onto small wooden slates hung with hooks. Hong would sit and watch me and tend to the patients he had. Occasionally, he would correct me; he encouraged me by saying that the more I practiced, the more I would understand. Many times he had me practice standing meditation (*pi quan*), standing on one leg and then the other, alternately for four hours in the hallway. Finally, at noon, he would give me money to buy lunch for both of us at a noodle cart on the corner.

5) Years later, Hong's office front takes on a different look.
6) Robert Yu (center) with fellow students San Jyan and Chou Jintsai at the elementary school gym where they practiced.

7) Hong with his senior students and a group of young boxers at the Taipei City tournament in 1970. Hong entered three students and took three first-place awards.

Hong was an uncomplicated man with a big heart. He smiled a lot and liked to laugh and he got very nervous when he had to talk in front of a large group of people. In Taiwan, Hong was considered a master of xingyi. The Chinese martial art societies knew the teachers he trained under, and his lineage. Hong liked to fight and his reputation as a fighter was considerable. Once he deflated a long-standing feud between two martial arts schools by saying he would fight both the teachers. He was well-known for his xingyi trained fighters who won in national tournaments. His girth, thick wrists, gravelly voice, and having the surprising speed of a big man gave everyone pause when they considered this man's capabilities.

The Five Elements and the Five Fists

The xingyi form that I was doing in the hallway of Hong's office some 32 years ago is called the *wuxing*. It is the most important form in the xingyi style. Wuxing means "five elements," represented by metal, water, wood, fire, earth.[1]

The five elements theory appears in many places in the Chinese world view; in its art, literature, philosophy, Daoist cosmology, and traditional medicine. These five elements are not viewed as static entities but represent the phases that energy moves through. Energy changes; it emerges, grows, and expands. It also diminishes, ebbs, and contracts. It can be solid as a rock or as wispy as a cloud. When energy moves and reaches its zenith, it is closest to its demise. It transcends as it begins to rise or begins

8) The five first-place winners pose with Hong at an "open" National Wushu Tournament in which all styles were eligible.

to fade. The five elements is a description of energy as it changes and evolves and these transitions are represented by the symbols metal, water, wood, fire, earth.[2]

Xingyi literally embodies the idea of energy change into its movements. Training body movement to use "internal" energy results in a different quality of motion than movement that does not train in this way. Movement that uses internal energy has more power than motion that uses simple force (as defined by Force = Mass x Speed). In fighting, the force typically used is generated by the combination of speed and muscle mass, so it follows that faster speed and larger muscles will result in greater impact. However, in xingyi training, the use of force is just the first step in understanding how to develop and use one's power. Real power comes from learning to use one's energy.

In xingyi, the forms are exercises that are designed to develop this "intrinsic" or internal energy. To develop internal energy one must be trained to: (a) align the spine in a variety of positions; (b) develop flexibility to increase the body's potential; (c) engage the waist (*gua*) (Yu, 2001:68, 70),[3] and (d) cultivate internal energy (*qi*) and use this energy with the conscious body movement (*fajing*).[4] These are the qualities of internal energy. All these actions must come together to create energy and when this energy is combined with force, it maximizes one's fighting intention. The student is taught to initiate action with a combination of force and energy. Force is thought of as square, linear and straight, while energy is visualized as round, circular and wavy.[5] Pure energy is utilized instinctively, as when a tiger pounces on a deer.

89

The genius of xingyi is in its synthesis of the five elements. The adaptation of the five elements theory of energy change to body movement has made xingyi famous among Chinese who otherwise would have had little interest in the martial arts.

The five fists form activates the five energies by practicing the movements and postures of the "five fists." The type of energy gathered for each of the five fists is characterized by these descriptive words:

- metal-fist: a splitting-cleaving action like an ax,
- water-fist: a drilling-boring action like a waterfall,
- wood-fist: a crushing-smashing action like a battering ram,
- fire-fist: a pounding-bursting action like a ball shot out of a cannon, and
- earth-fist: crossing fists with a swirling, corkscrew-like action on an axis.[6]

As stated above, xingyi's training is based on developing internal energy in movement. The postures of the five elements form follow these same ideas to gain this power. Each posture of the five fists:

- aligns the body structure—the head and neck with the spine, the spine with the hips, the legs and the feet;
- initiates action from a different angle requiring different muscles and tendons and ligament connections;
- achieves leverage through the waist (gua) action with grounding/rooting (Yu, 2001: 68);[7] and
- gathers the internal energy and properly retains and disperses it.

This classic five elements theory of energy change is divided into two phases: energy creation and energy destruction. These two phases are interpreted in xingyi's five elements theory by the order of the five fists' movements. In the creation sequence, the minerals of metal-fist vitalize the water-fist; then the water-fist nourishes the wood-fist which fuels the fire-fist; the fire-fist creates the earth-fist, and the earth-fist heats up to fuse into the metal-fist, and then the cycle starts over again.

The destruction sequence is cyclical as well: the metal-fist chops the wood-fist; the wood-fist defeats the earth-fist by covering it; the earth-fist absorbs the water-fist; the water-fist extinguishes the fire-fist; and the fire-fist melts the metal-fist, and so on.

Master Hong Yixiang said that the earth-fist has the mechanics of the other four five elements fists. Earth represents the unifying element, a transitional phase between the other four phases. From its center axis, it can create and destroy the other four fists.

The five fists postures put the body in optimum positions to strike or neutralize an opponent from different directions. A changing position is practiced as the movement of energy responding to changing circumstances. Special attention is given to practicing movements from one posture to another posture, such as the transitions between metal-fist and water-fist or between fire-fist and earth-fist or between any combination of fists. An awareness of the transitions between postures trains the feet

9) Hong serving as an official judge at a National Wushu Tournament.

10) Mr. Lin, who proved to be one of Hong's top xingyi fighters, wins in his weight division. He wears the famous "Yen Ping" T-shirt, the name of a district in Taipei with the city's oldest Taiwanese neighborhood where Hong live and taught.

11) Another one of Hong's top student's, Say Jyan, wins a match in Taipei, 1971. He later moved to Japan where he became a famous teacher.

and hands to move together with the waist (*gua*) and promotes smooth and continuous motions. This type of exercise prepares the xingyi student for spontaneous reaction to the vicissitudes of a fight.

Amazingly, xingyi's "five fists" and the five standard punches in American boxing, two distinct traditions from opposite ends of the world, are basically the same five punches. The metal-fist is a jab, the water-fist is right and left uppercuts, the wood-fist is a straight punch or an overhand punch or a cross punch, the fire-fist is a hook.[8] The five elements is practical, with clear parallels to Western boxing. However, an important difference is that while the five standard punches in American boxing represent boxing tactics, the five elements' "five fists" represent training postures.

The creation sequence is a progression of punches or combinations. In the creation sequence a jab (metal-fist), is followed by an uppercut (water-fist), followed by a straight or an overhand or a cross punch (wood-fist), followed by a hook (fire-fist), followed by the earth-fist.

This offensive routine is followed by defensive maneuvers. The destruction sequence is a series of counters. The counter to a metal-fist (jab) is a fire-fist (hook); the counter to a fire-fist is a water-fist (uppercut); the counter to a water-fist is an earth-fist; the counter to an earth-fist is a wood-fist (a straight or an overhand or a cross punch); the counter to a wood-fist is a metal-fist (jab).

12) Hong and his boys hit the streets. They are on way to TTV television studio for a live show about Hong's school.

13) Say Jyan and Ya Dan practice *san shou*, xingyi's equivalent to taijiquan's "push-hands."

14) Robert Yu and another one of Hong's top students, Chou Jintsai, sip tea at River Park after a workout in 1985. Hong often frequented this park.

Thus this sequence of energy creation and destruction can be practiced as a boxing strategy of offensive and defensive maneuvers; each fist can follow a natural order into another fist, or a combination of consecutive punches, and each thrown fist has a counter punch. Thus the metaphysical idea of the wuxing, of energy creation and destruction, can serve as a practical sparring routine.

As with many ideas from Chinese antiquity, there has been controversy over the five elements theory. A quote of the late Han Dynasty *Wen Zi* text serves as an apt caveat for any boxer who fails to adjust boxing strategy to the realities of a fight.

Metal may overcome wood, but with one ax a man cannot cut down a whole forest. Earth may overcome water, but with a single handful, one cannot dam up a river. Water may overcome fire, but with no more than a cup of it one cannot put out a large conflagration.

– Needham, 1956: 260

When performed, five elements movements appear to be linear; however, with continual practice the student becomes aware of the circles, the coiling springs, and the band springs that are to be found in the motion of the waist, the legs and the arms. It is then that the xingyi practitioner can discover the energy characteristic of the five elements within one's body.

Xingyi training will transform the body. Doing the classical five elements form, one practices initiating energy from both the right and the left sides of the body. Xingyi drills are designed to change the old body, to overcome habitual tendencies and imbalances and to restore the symmetry and balance of the body to its original form.

After months of practicing the five elements and the other xingyi forms, every joint in my body seemed to be affected. At different times my shoulders and legs ached, then my hips and ankles were sore. Hong said that this was a good sign, and that the stiffness in the joints would go away with more practice; that the benefits of xingyi take time, and that the feeling of soreness would be replaced by a feeling of strength and flexibility.

Many years have passed since I learned with Hong. At the end of my stay, he said to me that I had trained hard; that I needed more time to absorb all that he had shown me; and more time to digest all that he taught me. Hong said that the practice of the five elements form is the key to understanding xingyi's gift. It is with the enduring practice of the five elements form that these ancient lessons are passed on.

Gathering after evening class, June 2002. Front row: Paula Robbins, R. Yu's daughter Clarissa, Robert Yu, Yu's son Dayton; 2nd row, Francisco Rodriquez, Mary Wheeler, Matt Cramer-Carlson; 3rd row, Brad Breunig, and William Annis.

Metal Demonstrating: Robert Yu.

Water (top) & Wood (bottom)

Fire

Earth

Destruction Sequence

Hong's interpretation of the techniques of each of the five elements was limitless. He routinely showed ten possible uses of each element in different situations. The sequence of techniques demonstrated here is a typical interpretation of the "destruction" sequence. Notice that the boxing combinations and counters of the five element form have a natural flow. In this example, metal chops wood, fire melts metal, water extinguishes fire, earth absorbs water, and wood penetrates earth.

Demonstrating: James Gonzales (black) and Alec Stanley (white).

Metal (right) chops wood (elbow to face).   Beginning of fire (left) melting metal.

End of fire (left) melts metal.   Middle of water (left) extinguishes fire.   Beginning of water (left) extinguishes fire.

| End of water (left) extinguishes fire. | Beginning of earth (right) absorbing water. | End of earth (right) absorbing water. |

Beginning of wood (left) penetrates earth.

End of wood (left) penetrates earth.

Acknowledgments

The author thanks readers: Pam Heggesta, Peter Wolff, Tricia Yu and Victor Yu; xingyi teacher: Frank Juszczyk (Silver City, NM); students: William Annis, Matt Cramer-Carlson, Fawn Durny, James Gonzales, Dale Ivarie, Tiffany Kelly, Ben Liu, Niki McGlathery, Nile Ostenso, Lynette Penewell, Aaron Richie, Paula Robbins, Frank Rodriguez, Alex Stanley, Ted Swayer, Mary Wheeler, Clarissa YuDayton Yu and Kai Yu; Minneapolis students: Craig Lewis, Joe Bozicevich and Jumba Mugabi; Washington, D.C. student: Jim Tucker; Art Work: Kai Yu; Photos: Peter Wolff and Niki McGlathery.

References

Miller, D., and Cartmell, T. (1994). *Xing Yi nei gong: Xing Yi health maintenance and internal strength development*. Pacific Grove, CA: High View Publications.

Needham, J. (1956). *Science and civilisation in China, volume 2*. Cambridge: Cambridge University Press

Olson, S. (Trans.) (1994). *The intrinsic energies of t'ai chi ch'uan: Chen Kung series volume two*. Saint Paul, MN: Dragon Door Publications.

Smith, R., and Pittman, A. (1989). *Hsing-I: Chinese internal boxing*. Charles E. Tuttle Company.

Tian, Y., and Yao, G. (Winter 2001). Yang's taiji boxing secrets. *Qi Magazine*, *11*(4): 18-29.

Yu, R. (2001). American boxing and Chinese Xing Yi: A comparison. *Journal of Asian Martial Arts*, 10(3): 64-75.

Jones, M. (October, 2001). Xing Yi quan five elements with Luo De Xiu. *Internal Martial Arts*, p. 10.

Notes

[1] There are photographs of Luo Dexiu doing the wuxing form. Luo studied with Master Hong during the same period as I did. He is the number one teacher from Hong's school and a master of both xingyi and bagua. Our paths crossed briefly in 1985 when I returned to Taiwan to study xingyi staff form with Master Hong and bagua with Chou Jintsai.

[2] The term *wuxing* also has been translated to mean the five phases (Needham, 1956: 244). To quote: "As Chhen Meng-Chia says, the five 'elements' were five powerful forces in ever-flowing cyclical motion, and not passive motionless fundamental substances."

[3] The *gua* is the action of the pelvic girdle and hip joint area to coil and spring when initiating a punch or block.

[4] *Fajing* is the action that occurs when one's internal energy (*qi*) is combined with force (*li*).

[5] See Tian and Yao (2001: 18-29) for a good discussion of the internal system's interpretation of force vis-a-vis energy.

[6] See Olson (1994). Olson lists intrinsic energies used in taijiquan. These energies are shared by other Chinese internal systems. Here is a partial list: sticking, listening, receiving, neutralizing, raising, sinking, seizing, pulling, twisting, grasping, pushing, separating, opening, and closing.

[7] To ground and to root are closely related concepts that connect the feet to the earth as the source of power. Xingyi emphasizes grounding and rooting in its training.

[8] Xingyi boxers rely on hand techniques, but it should be noted that the wuxing form has leg movements that train the feet for kicks, sweeps, trips and the like.

Insights From
The Home of Xingyiquan

by Stanley E. Henning, M.A.

Spear practice in Taigu city. Map of China. Shanxi province is shown in dark grey.
All photos courtesy of Stanley Henning.

Introduction

I started practicing xingyiquan during an Army assignment to Taiwan between 1970-1972. My teacher, Dr. Wu Chaoxiang, a patient and generous man, was from Shanxi Province. Studying both Yang style taijiquan and Shanxi Che style xingyiquan from Dr. Wu in Taiwan was a wonderful, unforgettable experience. Little did I realize then that it would be a defining moment in my life and the start of a long adventure that would ultimately take me to the home of xingyiquan and beyond.

Visiting the home of xingyiquan was an important goal, but another aspect of Shanxi Province that equally fired my imagination was the fact that it is one the most prolific repositories of Chinese culture in the country. Outstanding examples of art and architecture from as early as the 5th century are scattered throughout the Shanxi countryside. So, it was a combination of factors that spurred me on.

My contact with Shanxi martial arts in their natural environment began shortly after I crossed the Yellow River from Shaanxi in May 2000. After a winding bus ride through the bare loess hills, I arrived in the town of Ruicheng to spend the evening. Alighting from the bus, I caught a motorcycle (a major form of local one-man taxi service) to the Ruicheng Government hostel, which boasted a five star plaque—literally the place to stay in Ruicheng, which is the location of the Yongle Gong (Palace of Eternal Joy), a Daoist monastery famous for its incredible Yuan period (ca. 1262) wall murals. I explored Ruicheng's one main street that afternoon and saved the visit to Yonglee Gong for the next morning.

After a day of travel in China, I always enjoy a bowl of noodles or some other local goodies, a nice cold bottle of beer, and discussion with local residents. This might be in a small eatery or, as in this case, at a strategic point out on the sidewalk. As conversation touched on the martial arts, a local taxi driver offered to take me to the elementary school when school let out to see his son and classmates practice martial arts. It was a rewarding experience. The kids practiced hard, and my driver friend noted that his son was a top contender in provincial competition. In fact, the father was investing heavily in his son's being a top national level martial artist. This was not unusual, especially after the 1970's international appearance of the movie "Shaolin Monastery" starring Li Lianjie, now known worldwide as Jet Li.

The next morning, I toured the Yongle Gong, a portion of which housed an art center, where students came from all over to develop a foundation in traditional painting using exact scale copies of the wall murals as their models. From Ruicheng I took a winding mountain road north to Haizhou, birthplace of Guan Yunchang (Guan Yu, Guan Gong), the Three Kingdoms (220-265 C.E.) hero later deified variously as the God of War and patron saint to Buddhist monasteries, businessmen, and others. Symbolically depicted with a powerful red visage and long, black beard, he is considered the epitome of strength, loyalty, and sincerity. Originally erected in 589 C.E., the Haizhou Emperor Guan Temple is a magnificent structure and the grand ancestor of temples dedicated to Guan Yu.

From Haizhou, I traveled to Yuncheng, the main city in this historical salt producing area, located on the main north-south rail line through the heart of Shanxi Province. In Yuncheng, I purchased a train ticket and bided my time outside the station at an open-air meat cake vendor's stand. Here I enjoyed a pleasant interlude, conversing with local residents and picking up a few phrases of their dialect. All the while, standing by us was a large majestic statue of Guan Yu on horseback carrying his famous "Blue Dragon Crescent Moon Big Halberd," according to tradition his weapon of choice. Over the ages, Guan Yu's big halberd became a symbol of martial prowess, while depictions of him with a copy of the *Spring and Autumn Annals* in his hand reflected his civil or intellectual side.

I took the train north from Yuncheng to China's best-preserved walled city, Pingyao, where I spent a couple of days taking in the sights both in and around the city. The impressive city wall is 33 feet high (10 meters), 16.5 feet wide (5 meters), and 4 miles (6.4 kilometers) in circumference. Big East, West, and South Streets converge around the centrally located city tower. This area contains the largest concentration of Ming (1368-1644) and Qing (1644-1911) period commercial buildings. One of these buildings is home to the North China Three Heroes Protection Bureau Museum, filled with mid-Qing period protection bureau paraphernalia, including weapons, escort consignment containers, vehicles, and historical material emphasizing three local martial artists: "Spirit Spear" Wang Zhengqing, "Iron Legs" Zuo Erba, and Yiquan proponent Dai Erlu. Protection bureaus run by martial artists

101

Left: In the city of Ruicheng, an acquaintance with his son and friend with their spears.
Right: Yuncheng city—a meat pie stand and its happy owner.

were especially prevalent in north China from the mid- to late-Qing period, when Shanxi Province was an important center of banking and commerce.

There are also numerous historical sites well worth seeing in the vicinity of Pingyao. One should not miss Shuanglin Monastery, an incredible repository of Ming period Buddhist clay statuary; and Zhenguo Monastery, maintaining its original appearance since its construction in 963 C.E. I reached the latter by riding 7.5 miles (12 kilometers) in a motorcycle sidecar.

The evening before departing Pingyao, I tasted a local dish with a name I cannot forget–Cat's Ears. I had eaten chicken feet and pig's ears before, but this was a first. I amused the shop owner by asking him where he got all the cats to manage this delicacy. With both embarrassment and a sense of relief, I discovered that the "cat's ears" were actually a pasta formed by pressing small pieces of dough into their namesake shape, boiling them like noodles, and adding a sauce. Tasty indeed! I recommend them.

From Pingyao I moved north into the heart of xingyiquan territory, Qixian and Taigu. Qixian is dotted with enormous walled mansions, one of which, the Qiao Family Mansion, was the site of the movie "Hang the Big Red Lantern High," about the plush, secluded lifestyle of the wealthy even into the early 20th century.

At another mansion, this of the Qu Family, I met Mr. Wang Yi, assistant museum head, who practiced what he claimed was the original form of xingyiquan. His demonstration revealed considerable emphasis on maintaining erect posture, developing inner energy through interaction between breath and movement, and emitting sound with release of force. It did not seem to emphasize going through numerous form practicing routines that one sees in the later styles of xingyiquan, including the Che style I learned and is practiced in nearby Taigu. Although my impression was admittedly gained only by "viewing the flowers from horseback," it seemed like this early version of xingyiquan contained the basics, while the five elements and twelve animals routines were additions over time.

Left: statue of Guanyu, on horseback with his halberd. Right: art students practicing to preserve a precious heritage by copying murals from the Yongle Gong in Ruicheng.

From Qixian I moved on to Taigu, finally arriving at the home of the Shanxi Che style xingyiquan that I had studied in Taiwan 30 years earlier. Upon arrival I immediately went to the nearest public phone kiosk and asked for directions to a local martial arts association. When I was asked "what style?," I knew I was in the right place. I was given the name and address of Mr. Yang Fansheng, who lived on the outskirts of Taigu. Though somewhat surprised to see a foreigner at his door, Mr. Yang graciously invited me in, and asked me to be seated. When he learned why I had come to Taigu, he immediately began to make a number of phone calls and, within about an hour, over half a dozen individuals had converged upon his residence. The rest of the afternoon and into the evening, when the group took me to a local hotel for dinner, was spent discussing xingyiquan. Naturally, everyone was interested in how I came to study xingyiquan—who my teacher was and so forth. As it turned out, they all knew of my teacher, Dr. Wu Chaoxiang, who left Mainland China in the wake of the Communist takeover and later immigrated to Brazil, where he set up a traditional Chinese medical practice and taught taijiquan and xingyiquan. They were proud of his role in introducing xingyiquan overseas, and he was duly recorded among the students of Bu Xuekuan (1876-1971), a student of Che Yizhai (1833-1914).

One thing I was introduced to prior to departing for dinner was basic training with a large bamboo pole about twelve feet long and nearly three and a half inches in diameter at the base. This was clearly meant as a test of strength and endurance, while attempting to execute thrusts accurately. This gives credence to the view found in the earliest xingyiquan manuals of the intimate relationship between xingyiquan and spear practice. In fact, spear practice such as Six Harmonies Spear (*Liuhe Qiang*) is integrated with the training in other traditional styles of boxing such as bajiquan. In traditional martial arts, the staff is considered at the forefront—it provides a foundation in body, hand, and foot movement—but the spear is called "king" because it is considered the most difficult to defend against.

Left: Entrance to the Protection Agency Museum in Pingyao city. Center: Clay guardian figure at Shuanglin Monastery. Right: Stone tablet in Pingyao Museum courtyard erected by warlord military and civil governor from 1911 through the 1930's, Yan Xishan. It reads: "All types who are harmful to the people—such as corrupt officials, evil gentry and local bullies—must be eliminated in accordance with legal procedures."

Dinner was great and toasts of clear liquor followed one after another. Early the next morning I watched a xingyiquan class held on a side street. There was a mix of students of various ages and both sexes, and everyone was practicing different techniques, including one sturdy young fellow who was kicking trees and another practicing spear. The instructor was Cheng Suren, the local xingyiquan historian, calligrapher, and seventh-degree martial artist in the new Chinese martial arts ranking system. He was research assistant in the provincial historical gazetteer office in Taigu. He had recently updated and republished a *Complete Book of Xingyiquan* by his 90-year old teacher, Wu Dianke. A month before I passed through, he had published a three volume (1,344 pages) historical novel, *Xingyi Grand Master*. He was also quite busy as head of the Shanxi Xingyiquan Cultural Research Center, which had a number of products available such as DVD's and other publications. Before I departed Taigu, Cheng Suren and Yang Fansheng accompanied me to the White Pagoda, a Song period monument (ca. 1090), from which one can get a panoramic view across Taigu city. They asked me to contact my teacher in Brazil and invite him back to his old home and the home of xingyiquan.

I boarded the train and went on to the provincial capital of Taiyuan. In 1900, this and much of Shanxi was a major scene of anti-foreign activity, which reached its climax in the famous Boxer Uprising. Then Shanxi Governor Yu Xian supported the boxers and personally ordered the execution of numbers of foreigners and Chinese Christian converts. As for the boxers, most were poor and ignorant and

Left: The author with Yang Fansheng and Cheng Suren in front of White Pagoda. Center: In Taigu city, a young girl keeps flexible through a daily regime of streatching exercises. Right: An iron warrior at the Jin Memorial Hall located in the provincial capital of Taiyuan. Below: The author with Mr. Wang Yi in front of Mansion Museum in Qixian city; view inside the masion courtyard.

their makeshift martial arts training, supposedly enhanced by magic talismans, proved no match for the modern weapons of the Eight Nation Expedition that converged on Beijing to subdue them.

Among the sights to see in Taiyuan is the Jin Memorial Hall (*Jinci*), a large complex of numerous structures, some built earlier, but most during the Northern Song period (960-1127). The most famous is the Heavenly Mother Hall, with its 43 beautiful, lifelike clay sculptures of maids in waiting. For the martial artist, there is the Iron Man Terrace in the center of the complex, with its four life-size cast-iron martial guardian figures (ca. 1097).

This large Tibetan-style Taihuai Monastery complex is located on Mount Wutai.

From Taiyuan I took a three-day trip north to Mount Wutai, a large area dotted with Buddhist monasteries, a couple dating to the Tang period (618-960). Mount Wutai is considered one of China's four most important Buddhist mountains. Interestingly, Mount Song with its Shaolin Monastery is not one of these, but is, instead, the central of China's five sacred mountains (based on geomancy, not Buddhism). In fact, the martial monks of Mount Wutai led by Monk Zhenbao are recorded in history for their brave last stand against an invading Jin (Jürched) army (1127-1279). There are also a number of legendary stories of martial monks and others on Mount Wutai, and it was recognized along with Mount Song (location of Shaolin Monastery in Henan) and Mount Funiu in Henan for its monk soldiers.

My trip through the home of xingyiquan ended at Datong in the north, near a segment of the Great Wall and the Inner Mongolia Autonomous Region. Datong is home to a couple of magnificent monasteries. One, the Lower Huayan Monastery, contains beautiful Buddhist clay statuary from the Liao Dynasty (916-1125) and nearby are the Yungang Grottos with stone statuary (over 50,000 carvings produced between 460-524).

My greatest insight was to see how the martial arts in general and xingyiquan in particular are among the many colorful pieces that make up the cultural and historical mosaic of Shanxi Province, and it was the people I met along the way who helped bring all these pieces to life and make the experience unforgettable.

Bibliography

Henning, S. (1999). Martial arts myths of Shaolin Monastery: The giant with the flaming staff. *The Chenstyle Journal*, 5(1).

Li Chi. (1974). *The travel diaries of Hsu Hsia-ko*. Hong Kong: Chinese University of Hong Kong, note 17, 253-254.

chapter 9

Che Style Xingyiquan in Taiwan as Taught by Dr. Wu Chaoxiang

by Stanley E. Henning, M.A.

Left to right: Dr. Wu Chaoxiang (1917-2000); performing a technique imitating the action of a monkey; the Legislative Yuan building partially blocked by a section of the National Taiwan University Hospital. *Picture taken July 2, 2005 by Allen Timothy Chang. All photos courtesy of S. Henning, except where noted.*

Learning xingyiquan from Dr. Wu Chaoxiang (Wu Chaohsiang, 1917-2000) in Taiwan in 1971-72 was a defining experience in my life. Dr. Wu was from Shanxi Province, the home of xingyiquan. He was a student of Mr. Bu Xuekuan (1876-1971) of Taigu County. Master Bu studied under Che Yizhai (1833-1914) whose family name is associated with this particular xingyiquan style. Dr. Wu taught this Shanxi Che style, one of the three dominant xingyiquan styles, the other two being the Hebei and Henan styles.

Dr. Wu was one of a number of Mainland Chinese who gathered every Sunday in the courtyard of the old Legislative Yuan (literally "law establishing court") in Taipei to chat and pass on their knowledge to an interested younger generation. They represented the heart of the Mainland martial arts community that migrated to Taiwan in 1949. As such, they offered a rich cross section of the various styles practiced in China. Among them were Mr. Ju Hao, who had studied Hebei style under Sun Lutang in the Central Martial Arts Institute, established in Nanjing in 1927 (Green & Svinth, 2003: 23-24), and Mr. Zhou Jichun (Jian Nan), who was the historian among the group (Smith, 1974: 113-121). In 1972, Dr. Wu immigrated to Rio de Janeiro, Brazil, where he founded The Chinese Cultural Institute and taught until his death. He has a large following in Brazil, where he was considered to be an ambassador of Chinese culture, and among his many students is Nelson Ferriera, head of the Zhong Yi Kung Fu Association in Madison, Wisconsin.

Classic Shanxi Che Style

The original Shanxi Che style xingyiquan appears quite plain and straightforward, especially in comparison with some of the "enhanced" performance versions of xingyiquan, which have been developed recently to accommodate the demands of official sports program competition and popular preferences in China's rapidly evolving society. The Che style is practically oriented. Dr. Wu's teacher, Bu Xuekuan, is quoted as saying, "Fighting technique relies completely on the flow of inner energy, unique formation of spherical force, spring power, and responsive release of force and control of an opponent." He believed in picking the best techniques that others in the martial arts community displayed and was known for his "swallowing lion hand" (*shi tun shou*) (Shanxi Wenshi, 1992: 305).

From the start, Dr. Wu's students spent a considerable amount of time perfecting the basic, stable three point stance (*santi shi*), which gives rise to all forms and routines. This stance emphasizes the essential elements of posture, balance, and coordination necessary to effectively maneuver and issue force. It represents the simultaneous combination of defense and offense and is a visible manifestation of one's cultivation of three inner combinations (mind, energy, and power) and three external combinations (shoulders and waist, elbows and knees, and hands and feet), or six combinations (*liuhe*) (Wu, 1969, Vol. 36: 44).[1] In fact, Six Combination Boxing (*Liuhequan*) was among the earliest names for what has since come to be called xingyiquan.

Left: Dr. Wu's xingyiquan teacher, Bu Xuekuan (1876-1971).
Right: Dr. Wu in three point stance.

Dr. Wu also taught two other stances, the supreme void stance (*wuji shi*) and the life-principle stance (*hunyuan zhuang*). The former is a lead in to the three point stance, while the latter is practiced to mentally focus energy and direct force as reflected in the phrase, "fist yet no fist, intent yet no intent, in the midst of no intent is real intent" (Sun, 1970b: 28). The student must come to his own conclusions when interpreting phrases such as this. My view is that this refers to developing spontaneity in responding to an opponent's release of force. It demands a cleared mind, focused on the situation of the moment.

"Fighting technique relies completely on the flow

of inner energy, unique formation of spherical

force, spring power, and responsive release of

force and control of an opponent."

Left to right: Dr. Wu in life-principle stance and demonstrating spear techniques for his class.

From the three point stance, students went on to study the five element forms: metal/ splitting, wood/crushing, water/drilling, fire/exploding, and earth/crossing. Needless to say, these are imperfect descriptions of the techniques, which only become clear with actual practice. After practicing the individual five element forms, students tied them together with the lianhuan solo routine and then practiced two duo routines called the little five flower pounder and five element pounder, both of which pit the techniques against each other. However, beyond these two different two-person routines, students did not dwell on a dogmatic interaction between the five elements, as this would have taken the flexibility of mind/intent out of xingyiquan.

Dr. Wu emphasized control as an important principle. Students practiced grasping/seizing, particularly of the wrists and elbows, as an essential xingyiquan fighting technique, key to controlling an opponent, and enhancing the effectiveness of one's own release of force, and reflective of Bu Xuekuan's "swallowing lion hand" (Yang, 1984), where simultaneous seizing and pulling force from one hand reinforces one's striking force with the other. Dr. Wu also executed his splitting form with a clenched fist and twisting motion, the combination of which enhanced the form's effectiveness. The twist upon contact increases the effect on the target and, at the same time, reduces the impact to the practitioner.

Dr. Wu And Five Elements
1) metal / splitting, 2) wood / crushing,
3) water / drilling, 4) fire / exploding, 5) earth / crossing

Students supplemented five element form training with spear practice. One early source (ca. 1735) relates how a member of the Shanxi Ji family (now known as Ji Longfeng) developed liuhequan from existing spear techniques as a means of self-defense in peacetime (Wu, 2000: 9). A more common view, expressed by others, including Ming Dynasty general Qi Jiguang, was that barehanded boxing styles were considered the foundation for weapons practice; however, when one becomes familiar with the five element forms, one can clearly discern a relationship, regardless of whether the spear or the boxing came first. Spear practice does assist in coordinating arm, leg, and waist, or whole-body (not merely upper body) movement in developing the release of force.

From the five elements, students moved on to practice the twelve animal forms common to the Shanxi and Hebei styles: dragon, tiger, monkey, horse, snake, rooster, swallow, hawk, alligator, tai,[2] eagle, and bear. Each of these animals corresponds to actual and derived fighting characteristics and, again, one may vary such interpretations through observation and practice:

Dr. Wu And Twelve Animals

1) dragon, 2) tiger, 3) monkey, 4) horse, 5) snake, 6) rooster,
7) swallow, 8) hawk, 9) alligator, 10) taixing, 11) eagle, 12) bear.

Dragon	龍	long	undulates to seize and throw an opponent.
Tiger	虎	hu	exhibits preparedness and pounces on its prey.
Monkey	猴	hou	is nimble and quick.
Horse	馬	ma	strikes with both hooves.
Snake	蛇	she	breaks through like separating the grass in its path.
Rooster	鷄	ji	displays multifaceted combativeness.
Swallow	燕	yan	swoops low scooping up.
Hawk	鷂	yao	can swoop in and strike from the flank.
Alligator	鼉	tuo	displays strength in its forearms/elbow.
Tai	鳥	tai	combines a deflective sweep and thrust with both fists.
Eagle	鷹	ying	mercilessly seizes its prey.
Bear	熊	xiong	is steady and swats or crushes its opponents.[3]

The author studying xingyi's protective pounder two-person routine with Dr. Wu in the early 1970s. In this mini-sequence, Dr. Wu is on the offensive, first blocking downward with his left hand while simultaneously kicking the attacker in the shins, and then stomping in to incapacitate and prevent escape with a palm strike to the forehead.

"Three fists, two ends"
technique based on how a mule cart driver
maneuvers a short whip handle.

Students practiced the twelve animal forms in the same manner as the five element forms, except for the rooster, which warranted an individual short routine called the fooster form four techniques. Students then learned the twelve animal solo routine or mixed form fist (*za shi chui*), and finally the twelve animal two-person routine or protective pounder (*an shen pao*).

As one of his favorite combination techniques, Dr. Wu also described "three fists, two ends" (*san quan liang ba*) as a practical defense based on how a Shanxi mule cart driver maneuvers a short whip handle. "Three fists" comprises a quick right-left-right sequence. The first two are sweeping deflections to clear a path for the third, which is the inward punch. Essentially, this is a combination of two deflections and a punch. The "two ends" represent the two ends of a cart driver's whip handle. The movement is a single handed jab and swat—one back handed jab to the solar plexus with the shorter back end of the handle and a quick flip upward and swat across the length of the face with the longer front end.

Learning xingyiquan under Dr. Wu was an unforgettable experience to know an outstanding human being and become familiar with a fascinating element of one of the world's oldest cultures. In the final analysis, no single book, much less chapter, will really fully open the door to this or any other style of martial art. The real secrets are only revealed through human interaction and individual insight.

Notes

[1] The following is another, more colorful way found in the manuals to describe the six combinations: legs of the rooster, body of the dragon, upper arms of the bear, grasp of the eagle, embrace of the tiger, and sound of thunder (*lei sheng*) (like the kiai or shouts in Japanese karate, Chinese martial artists also emitted sounds when releasing force) (Bao, 1971: 40; Jiang, 1970a: 8-9). According to Jiang Rongqiao, in the early 20th century teachers dropped the "sound of thunder" as uncultured. However, the sound of thunder, or "kiai" (comprised of the Chinese characters *qi* [vital energy] and *he* [unite], as it is still called in Japanese, was considered to be an important psycho-physiological phenomenon—a factor in the focus of vital energy in the release of force and, at the same time, it could distract one's opponent.

[2] The tai (taixing) is somewhat of a mystery animal. I was told it was an extinct bird. The latest "official" version claims it is a fish (Wu, 2000: 186). However, the only meaningful explanation is to describe the movement of the form: both fists, hanging naturally, swing together, cross, rise above the forehead, separate and swing out and down, and (1) cross again at waist level, fists up, or (2) fists together and up, but not crossing, come together at waist level.

[3] The Henan style lists only ten animals: dragon, tiger, monkey, horse, snake, rooster, swallow, hawk, eagle, and cat. The Henan style adds the cat, but drops the tai, alligator (the small Chinese alligator is now nearly extinct), and bear. However, Henan

proponent, Bao Xianting, demonstrates a number of combination eagle-bear forms in his manual (Bao, 1971: 46). On the other hand, I practiced one movement/technique in the Lianhuan solo routine called wildcat climbs the tree (*li mao shang shu*) (Sun, 1970a: 40-42). So, there are clearly some exceptions to the generalized descriptions of what constitutes the corpus of the various xingyiquan styles.

Glossary

an shen pao	安身炮
Hun Yuan Zhuang	渾元樁
kiai	氣合
Ji Longfeng	姬龍峰
Lei Sheng	雷聲
Li Mao Shang Shu	狸貓上樹
liuhe	六合
San Quan Liang Ba	三拳兩把
santi shi	三體勢
shi tun shou	獅吞手
wu ji shi	無極勢
xingyiquan	形意拳
Za Shi Chui	雜式捶

Five Elements	五行	wuxing
metal	金	jin
wood	木	mu
water	水	shui
fire	火	huo
earth	土	tu
splitting	劈	pi
crushing	崩	beng
drilling	鑽	zhuan
exploding	炮	pao
crossing	横	heng

Bibliography – Chinese

Bao Xianting (1971). *Xingyiquan manual.*

Jiang Rongqiao (1970a). *Illustrated xingyi mother boxing.*

Jiang Rongqiao (1970b). *Xingyi mixed form pounder-eight form fist combined.*

Shanxi Literature and History Editorial Committee (1992). *Shanxi literature and history selections.*

Sun Fuquan (1970a). *Xingyiquan study.*

Sun Fuquan (1970b). *Discussion of the true meaning of boxing.*

Wu Chaoxiang (1972). *The way to a strong body.*

Wu Chaoxiang (1971). *Brief introduction to xingyiquan.*

Wu Chaoxiang (1969). *Xingyiquan's basic techniques.*

Wu Dianke (2000). *Complete xingyiquan.*

Yang Jisheng (1984, April). *Shanxi xingyiquan duo practice: Six methods of free fighting.*

Yang Yingguang (1985). *Shanxi Che school of xingyiquan.*

寶顯廷 (1971).《形意拳譜》1936，台北：中華武術出版社。

姜容樵 (1970a).《寫真形意母拳》1930，台北：中華武術出版社。

姜容樵 (1970b).《形意雜式捶。八式拳合刊》1930，台北：中華武術出版社。

山西文史 (1992). 山西文史資料編輯編《山西文史精選》
　　　Vol. 10，太原：山西高校聯合出版社。

孫福全 (1970a).《形意拳學》1915，台北：中華武術出版社。

孫福全 (1970b).《拳意述真》1924，台北：中華武術出版社。

武朝相 (1972).《強身之道》台北：中華武術出版社。

武朝相 (1971).『形意拳簡介』《武壇》第一卷，第五期，13。

武朝相 (1969).『形意拳的基本功夫』上中下《太極拳研究專集》
　　　第三十四，三十六，三十九期，台北：中華書局。

吳殿科主編 (2000).《形意拳術大全》太原：山西人民出版社。

楊吉生口述, 張青貴, 張希貴整理 (1984 April).『山西形意拳對練：
　　　散手六法』《搏擊》34: 16-17, 20.

楊映光，杜世秀整理 (1985).《山西車派形意拳》太原：山西人民出版社。

chapter 10

One Source, Four Images
Fu Yonghui's Sixiang Boxing

by Shannon Kawika Phelps, M.A., M.Div.

Fu Yonghui.
All photographs courtesy of S. Phelps.

Introduction

In a previous article (Phelps, 1996), I discussed how Mark Bow Sim was instrumental in the evolution of the art of liangyiquan, developed by Fu Zhensong and refined by his son, Fu Yonghui (Fu Wing Fei).[1] This chapter shares some of the distinct features of *sixiangquan* ("four images fist"), the next link of the cycle that begins from the mysterious, umbral source—*wuji*.

Fu Yonghui was born in 1911 in Mapo Village, Henan Province, the birthplace of his father, the legendary Fu Zhensong. He soon began his own lifelong pilgrimage as a martial artist in his father's footsteps. He studied along with his father in Beijing with Jia Fengming (Jia Qishen), a renowned student of Dong Haiquan. Fu also studied with others in the rich baguazhang clique in Beijing. He learned swordsmanship from Li Jinglin ("Miracle Sword Li") and Guo Qifeng; bajiquan and spear with Li Shuwen ("God Spear Li"); bajiquan with Huo Diange (the last emperor's instructor); and taijiquan and xingyiquan with Sun Lutang. Next to his father, Fu was perhaps most influenced by Yang Chengfu. His taijiquan classmates included Yang's nephew Fu Zhongwen and Li Tianji, both of whom became famous Beijing grandmasters in their day.

117

Fu Yonghui giving a lecture on sixiangquan to a special session of the Guangzhou Wudang Arts Association, circa 1975. He is in the taiji stage demonstrating a vital point strike (*dianxue*) fundamental to the Fu system. The Chinese signs reads: *WUDANG taiji, bagua, xingyi, taiji, liangyi, sixiang, bagua.*

Fu Yonghui was one of the few sons of the great masters who stepped beyond the shadow of his father and established himself as a great master in his own right. During his fifty years as a martial arts master, Fu Yonghui was head instructor for the Guangdong Public Security Department, the Guangdong Province and Guangzhou City Sports Commissions, the Communist Party School, Zhongshan University, and the Guangdong Treasury Department and Military Academy. At the time of his death (April 25, 1993), forty years to the day from when his father was fatally stricken after a performance, Fu Yonghui was vice president of the Guangdong Martial Arts Association, vice president of the Guangzhou City Martial Arts Association, and president of the Guangzhou Martial Arts Association's Wudang Boxing Committee.

As part of the responsibility of being the lineage heir, Fu assigned himself the tough duty of codifying and systematizing the staggering volume of martial arts collected by the founding father of what became the Fu Family Wudang System. About fifty complete empty-hand and weapons forms have survived.

Fu Yonghui described the form *sixiangquan* as "the summation of the Fu family martial arts" (Fu, 1984). It is indeed a summary of the four major arts that form the hub of the Fu family system. It incorporates the essential elements of Fu style taijiquan, liangyiquan, xingyiquan, and baguazhang. It is not a watering down of these arts: in fact, it may be the most physically strenuous form of the entire system. At first glance, the form seems to be designed in four sections combining the essentials of the four arts, with simple transitions to link them together as one form. It is this, but much more. If the dragon palm bagua was the apex of Fu Zhensong's legacy, then sixiangquan deserves that distinction for Fu Yonghui's contributions. China's *Xin Xia* newspaper reported in 1978 in a special article on Fu that sixiangquan should be considered "a rare masterpiece of the century" (Zhai, n.d.).[2]

His son Victor Fu Shenglong now carries on the family arts in Vancouver, BC, Canada. Victor suggests that his father felt that the system needed completion if it was to follow the natural pattern of the *Book of Changes* (*Yijing*), as was the custom according to the Daoist traditions of the Wudang Temple. The classic Confucian formula paraphrased by Fu Yonghui reads:

> Taiji creates liangyi. Liangyi creates the sixiang,
> and the sixiang creates the bagua, from the
> bagua emerges the ten thousand possibilities.
> – Fu, 1984

Fu Yonghui's father, Fu Zhensong, created fighting fist forms for taiji, liangyi, and bagua, but the sixiang was absent, or not really absent but left unarticulated through a fist form like the others. Fu Wenxiu, Fu Yonghui's younger sister (Victor's aunt) and last living child of Fu Zhensong, stated in a personal interview in Guangzhou (October 12, 1997), that their father did create a sixiangquan form but that it was lost. Zhai Rongji, disciple and last appointed successor of Fu Zhensong, concurs. "The master did create a form called sixiangquan, but did not teach it to anyone. Fu Yonghui's form is not the same as his father's. The original form was lost" (interview, October 12, 1997).

Fu Yonghui corrected or completed the process by creating a form he called sixiangquan. The form was developed after years of researching and refining his father's legacy and completed in 1974. Not just four forms linked together, sixiangquan became greater than merely the sum of its parts. Yet, before describing just how this is so, let us step back for a moment and review the rational basis from the classical tradition through which the Fu family system draws its creative genius.

Left: Fu Yonghui, circa 1975. Middle: Victor Fu Shenglong, 1996.

The author with Fu Yonghui's youngest son, Fu Wenlong ("cultured dragon") in Guangzhou. Wenlong's art is very high but he speaks no English and does not run a formal school.

The Source

Juxtaposed to the Confucian schools who treated the Taiji as the Great Source were classical Chinese philosophical sects known as yin-yang schools which blossomed after the time of the famous proto-scientist and naturalist, Zou Yan.[3] They also used the *Yi Jing* system of dividing and multiplying, but their starting point was always Wuji—"the Void," rather than Taiji. Now, contrary to some Western observers' interpretation of the term, Wuji does not mean "nothing," "blank," or "empty." In fact, it means just the opposite!

Wuji could be more properly interpreted as "no-thing," that is, a state of being in which all "things" are so combined that they have no individual identity; no name = "no-thing." Perhaps it may be likened to the universe before the "Big Bang." Being unable to label a thing as distinct from any other thing does not infer a vacuum; it means that nothing can be identified independently of the whole, so "no-thing" is not the absence but the presence of all things unindividualized.

Consider light, such as the light that comes from the sun. For lack of a better term, we call it "white light." Actually it has no color at all—but is it colorless? If we lay out a prism, we discover that when this light is broken down it consists of all the colors of the rainbow. So, "white light" isn't the absence of color, but is the presence of all colors before they are separated and revealed as the colors we can name. Wuji is something like this. It is the source of "Being" before Being was recognized as such by our consciousness. It is not "the Grand Ultimate" or Taiji, but is before "the Grand Ultimate." It gives being to Being without having the property of being because it is the progenitor of Being.

If this sounds convoluted, remember that the Greeks had the same problem. In describing "the One" and "the Nous" in his philosophical construct of "origin," Plotinus (205?-270 CE) struggled with the same speculative language.[4] Historically, the difficulty has always been in attempting to discuss the source of our knowledge by making it the object of our knowledge. Or, if this helps, it is like sitting in a dark room trying to look at the battery of a flashlight, which is the source of its light, by holding the battery up before the beam of light. Of course, as we move the battery, the light goes out! Making the source of thought the object of rational, objective thought is equally fruitless, which is why we have created myths, legends, allegory, metaphoric language, poetry, and dance: to compensate for the shortcomings of pure logic. This is also why some Buddhist sects turned to koans. Wuji is not a vacuum but "everything" before it becomes "something." This pristine state can have no name, for as Zhuangzi argued, "The one and what I said about it make two . . ." (Watson, 1968: 43). A name can refer to a concept but cannot be the thing itself, so to name "The One" is to contradict oneself. Named, the Source becomes less than the subject of our being because it is then the object of our own fallible reflections.

Taiji

Taiji is translated as "Grand Ultimate," "Great Ultimate," or "Being." The Chinese gave a name to Wuji after it is reflected through the prism of human consciousness and becomes the object of our thought as well as the source of our thoughts: Taiji, the philosophical repository of all potential. This concept is as far back as our logic can take us. This is why the Confucianists began here; they were less speculative than the Daoists, preferring to keep to practical issues of human endeavor. "No-Thing" has yet to be moved out from "the Source." However, the potential is there, as the Taiji contains, then reveals, the two potential forces, yin and yang, much as an egg contains the embryo of a chicken. Until it hatches, however, we do not call it a chicken; it only has the potential to become one!

Immersed in the Taiji, Mark Bow Sim uses the magic of the
Wudang to transform into the "White Snake" of Chinese folklore.

The Taiji is "center mass" of the "Big Bang." It is totally still, quiet, complete; it neither needs nor lacks anything. It is "Being" in the sense that it gives its Being to everything that comes after; it is the Great Beginning. As Laozi so beautifully refers to Dao, he was describing the Taiji:

> There was something formed out of chaos [Wuji],
> That was born before Heaven and Earth.
> Quiet and still! Pure and deep!
> It stands on its own and doesn't change.
> It can be regarded as the mother of Heaven and Earth.
> I do not yet know its name:
> I "style" it "the Way."
> Were I forced to give it a name, I would call it "the Great."
> – Hendricks, 1989: 77

While not wishing to take the analogy too far, if Wuji is the light before it passes through a prism, then perhaps Taiji is the prism itself—clear, yet through it is projected the opposite colors of yin and yang. Though itself clear and still, within Taiji there is potential for movement—for change. The Liangyi, the two primary elements of all Being, are balanced perfectly. "Change" is the result of the very first, primal, movement. What causes the very first movement? That's a theological question. In response to this question, Aristotle coined the term "the Unmoved Mover." In his response to the Neo-Aristotelians at the University of Paris, Thomas Aquinas declared this "Unmoved Mover" to be the God of scripture, but this is theological talk in which science can have no voice. The yin and yang theory has never been a theological pursuit, but a scientific one. Theology offers explanations of the "why" of the origin and goal and purpose of Being. Properly used, science avoids these questions and sticks to descriptions of "how" Being functions. There is support for this view from the scientific community:

> Objective knowledge provides us with powerful instruments for the achievements of certain ends, but the ultimate goal itself and the longing to reach it must come from another source. And it is hardly necessary to argue for the view that our existence and our activity acquire meaning only by the setting up of such a goal and of corresponding values. The knowledge of truth as such is wonderful, but it is so little capable of acting as a guide that it cannot prove even the justification and the value of the aspiration towards that very knowledge of truth. Here we face, therefore, the limits of the purely rational conception of our existence.
> – Einstein, 1950: 22

Quite cognizant of and more respectful of the boundaries between the two disciplines of theology and science than we have been in the West, the Chinese avoided the "why's" and stuck to "how," describing the process as we can know it through observation and prediction. Though we may not be able to verify "why," it is clear that movement did occur because we can observe the result.

Liangyi

Within the Taiji there was the potential for yang and that for yin. Yang is positive, active, and dynamic; yin is negative, inactive, and receptive. These are not "things," but are descriptive of an observable dynamic bipolar process. The obvious place to observe these two elements or attributes of process (Liangyi) was in the passing of day to night, of hot to cold, or sun to moon. Within our animate nature, this observation was reinforced by the presence of male and female, young and old, and life and death. At least in general terms, the whole world could be summed up as a reflection of a great duality that must have had its beginning in an even greater Oneness.

Sixiang

The Chinese continued to refine their descriptions by observing what they called Tai Yang (Greater Yang) and Tai Yin (Greater Yin), Xiao Yang (Lesser Yang) and Xiao Yin (Lesser Yin). These four "xiangs" ("images" or "likenesses") reflected both quality and quantity in the various observations of the dynamic process of yin and yang in flux. Everything seemed to have some yang and some yin; each varied in quantity and quality as yin rose toward yang or yang settled toward yxin.

The world was always in flux, predictable, but flux nonetheless. The sun and moon did not just come and go; they took hours to subside, one giving way to the other. The seasons were observed and recorded, and the four of them waxed and waned gradually one into the other, forming a great cycle. Tai Yang would be the sun at its peak; Xiao Yang would be the sun at its nadir; Tai Yin, the moon at its peak; Xiao Yin, the moon setting. And so it went, observation, calculation, prediction, and reflection.

Whatever process was at work in the cosmos seemed to be the same process observed in the country, the village, the family, and within the individual. We are all caught up in this same grand, mysterious process with its waxing and waning, its yang and yin. It seems to always be in motion yet, upon reflection, always complete. By following this Way of Heaven we have our model for the Way of Humankind:

> The Way of Heaven is like the flexing of a bow. The high it presses down; the low it raises up. From those with a surplus it takes away; to those without enough it adds on. Therefore the Way of Heaven—Is to reduce the excessive and increase the insufficient; The Way of Man—Is to reduce the insufficient and offer more to the excessive. Now, who is able to have a surplus and use it to offer to Heaven? Clearly, it's only the one who possesses the Way. Therefore the Sage—Takes actions but does not possess them; Accomplishes his tasks but does not dwell on them. Like this, is his desire not to make a display of his worthiness.

– Hendricks, 1989: 48

Bagua

It was a simple mathematical jump to realize that from the four images or "xiangs" one could formulate the eight possibilities or directions, the Bagua, from which the "Ten Thousand Things" could scatter and populate the whole earth.

The theory is not the complete scientific description of the evolution of humankind but is a quite useful description of how natural processes have always influenced one another and us—and still do. Each discipline of human endeavor has relied heavily on the predictableness of this basic worldview. Astronomers, farmers, economists, doctors, sailors, generals, and emperors have all staked their lives on the stability underlying the flux of yin and yang. By many other names, throughout the world, these two "forces" have aptly described the dynamic equilibrium of our existence, which is beyond our mortal control and in which we must all abide. From our reflections on nature around us, to reflections on our own human nature, the balance between these two elements (Liangyi) and the subsequent dichotomies has dictated our human course. To challenge the natural way of the immutable Dao is vanity; the wise among us have always warned against the futility of our arrogance when we abandon "the Way."

> For those who would like to take control of the world and act on it —
> I see that with this they simply will not succeed.
> The world is a sacred vessel;
> It is not something that can be acted upon.
> Those who act on it destroy it;
> Those who hold on to it lose it.
> With things — some go forward, others follow;
> Some are hot, others blow cold;
> Some are firm and strong, others submissive and weak;
> Some rise up while others fall down.
> Therefore the Sage:
> Rejects the extreme, the excessive, and the extravagant.
> – Hendricks, 1989: 81

In my old Stanford class notes I discovered this quote from my geology professor, Raymond Pestrong: "Each time we proceed in a direction contrary to that of natural processes, our action is met by a natural reaction, as though imposed as a warning." Humankind will not destroy the Earth. The Earth will survive and rejuvenate. It is our own species that we put in dire danger through our carelessness.

The Warrior

The warrior is but one more avid observer of this process of Nature. To be the victor, to survive, to thrive, the warrior must be clear about these matters because the stakes are ultimate ones: life or death. To miss the way Nature demonstrates this dynamic equilibrium is to miss the essence of those warnings, the "rules" by which the warrior lives or dies. Grasping the essentials, internalizing their meaning and practicing the way Nature evolves is to live. Clashing with "the Way," not heeding the warnings, is to break the "rules" of Nature, putting us in great danger. The Fu family's Wudang martial system is based on this principle: follow the way of Heaven, follow the Dao, and no enemy can stand against you!

> Man follows the Earth. Earth follows Heaven.
> Heaven follows the Dao.
> Dao follows what is natural.
> – Feng & English, 1972: #25

This has been a long way of saying that Fu Yonghui was doing more than creating a new form. On behalf of the warrior spirit, he was building a necessary bridge above the wide chasm between Liangyi and Bagua, reestablishing the complete cycle that follows Earth, which follows Heaven, which follows what is natural. In the case of the warrior, this ensures long life—if not long life, then victory, if not victory, then peace of mind in the face of every challenge.

Mark Bow Sim's impeccable Dragon Palm Bagua
form during a visit to author's San Diego school in 1996.

So the Blind May See

Do you remember the parable about the four blind men who described an elephant by feeling only one part of the elephant's body? One man feels the trunk and says an elephant is like a snake. Another feels the leg and declares an elephant is like the trunk of a tree. Still another feels the tail and says an elephant is like a whip. The fourth feels the ear and says an elephant is like the leaf of a large plant (or something to that effect). Well, another meaning of the character *xiang* is elephant! And that is actually quite helpful in analyzing what Fu was doing when he developed this form called sixiangquan.

Those who study taijiquan diligently, may after many years gain great understanding of the nature of Taiji. That is good, of course, but compared to the Fu family Wudang system this understanding would be similar to the blind man who only knows the elephant's leg. This is likewise true for anyone of the four major arts: taijiquan, liangyiquan, xingyiquan, and baguazhang. Knowing one of these arts is good, but knowing a "tree trunk" or a "snake" is not as good as knowing the whole elephant.

Taijiquan has the quality of Tai Yin, and knowing it is vital to the warrior. Liangyiquan is Xiao Yin, and its subtle changes increase the warrior's sensitivity to energy. Xingyiquan is Tai Yang, and it must be mastered for one to be a fully prepared warrior. Baguazhang is Xiao Yang, and it has unique subtleties that can make the fatal difference in a battle to the death. Together these arts explore every avenue of natural energy: explosive, empty, rising, sinking, transforming (following, returning), outward coiling, inward coiling, continuous motion, and perfect stillness. This is knowing the whole elephant. Sixiangquan is the summation of the Fu family arts in that every art is represented, every type of energy investigated, every type of defense anticipated, and every form of attack actualized.

THE FOUR ARTS
Taijiquan
Soft, pliable, internal stillness.
Liangyiquan
Soft, pliable, with rising, sinking, and coiling.
Xingyiquan
Explosive, solid, transforming.
Baguazhang
Continuous waves of movement, pulsing of hard and soft.

Of course each of these arts can claim elements of the others. What Fu was suggesting was that he could use each art as a vehicle to differentiate, emphasize and research its most explicit qualities. By first investigating the distinctions among these qualities through the four fist forms, the student could appreciate even more how they might be blended.

Taijiquan (Tai Yin)
By soft and pliable we do not mean limp. There is a continuous dynamic energy flowing throughout the body like the voltage in an electrical cord. The body is alive, receiving energy, interpreting it, and signaling back to the brain changes of tempo and the direction of incoming forces. Taijiquan is the most subtle; the waist coils and uncoils but the movement is in such a small circle that its mastery is lost on many who imitate the art. In Fu Taiji, for example, one can identify four distinct waist movements in "strum the lute" alone! Taijiquan seeks stillness; this does not mean immobility. There is no unnecessary movement that stirs up the inner qi and causes it to rise. By "still" we mean calm emotions; relaxed, dynamic muscles, and a feeling of circularity. It also

means to calm the environment around us so that any disruption of our auras is caused by the adversary, not by us. Useless movements of our own disturb the aura and make it difficult to "hear." It is like trying to hear subtle noises: if we are noisy, we cannot make the proper distinctions; if the environment is still, we hear every subtle vibration. This is the pure essence of yin.

Victor Fu performing Fu style taiji single whip.

Liangyiquan (Xiao Yin)

Liangyiquan retains all of the characteristics and requirements of taijiquan but extends them to the very limit. Its movements are larger but not so large as to disquiet the center and cause the qi to rise. It uses taijiquan's continuous motion and inner stillness but also emphasizes rising and sinking. It travels easily through the three basins and experiments with baguazhang's dragon coiling and cyclone sweeping. Yin is receding and the seed of yang is emerging.

Xingyiquan (Tai Yang)

Xingyiquan emphasizes following when the enemy retreats and returning when the enemy advances. If the enemy becomes like wood, we become metal; if he becomes fire, we become water. Tai Yang energy is explosive, solid, using splitting, crushing, drilling, and pounding. We imitate the process of yin and yang by producing the five elements. We imitate the forms of nature by observing the skills of animals. We transform from one to the other, becoming the superior "animal" as the enemy enters our defensive "death circle."

Baguazhang (Xiao Yang)

The Fu dragon is a mythical creature; strike him and he dissolves like a cloud; grasp him and he slips through your fingers. He swims and flies and attacks from the eight directions. He yields, merges, and blends, and just as suddenly becomes a great ocean wave that cannot be pushed back. Yin becomes yang and yang becomes yin. Front becomes back; back becomes side. The dragon rides the energy and fills the openings. Where as taijiquan is like water seeping through the cracks, baguazhang is like wind whipping through the hollows.

Fu Yonghui demonstrates liangyi single whip, circa 1975 (B-1-5).

Sixiangquan: Four Arts Become One

Sixiangquan links the four arts together, absorbs their unique energies, and creates a new spirit altogether. The form is formidable—108 movements.[5] Once internalized, if done at a moderate pace, it requires over twenty minutes to do. It begins like a train taking off from the station. After a qigong opening (movements 1 through 4) come the slow deliberate movements of Fu style taijiquan. Fu Taiji is deeper and more extended than Yang style, demonstrating full body flexibility. The breathing is fuller and is influenced by Sun Lutang's fajing elements (movements 5-23). Taijiquan transforms into liangyiquan. The liangyi adds rising and sinking and extended waist coiling, though the movements are still slow and even. Deeper breathing is required to compensate for the qi's desire to rise (movements 24-38). The transition to xingyiquan is quite obvious. The five elements and the twelve animals are all represented in a flurry of power, foot stamping, and fajing that challenges stamina to the limit. However, the real challenge is to maintain the principles and requirements of the "internal" arts and avoid the inclination to use brute force, or as Mark Bow Sim Sifu sometimes admonishes, "Don't turn it into Sumo!" (movements 39-82).

Victor Fu demonstrating liangyi
single whip in 1998 (C-1-5).

Xingyi Drills

demonstrated by Victor Fu.

Splitting (Pi)

Crushing (Peng)

Drilling (Duan)

Pounding (Pao)

Crossing (Heng)

| Dragon | Tiger | Horse | Reptile |

| Rooster | Hawk | Snake | Swallow |

| Monkey | Ostrich | Eagle | Bear |

Above: Grandmaster Fu Zhensong displays his bagua skills.
Below: Victor Fu demonstrating Fu Style bagua "body turning over."

There is no let-up. Next comes the twisting, whirling, spinning, and body turning of Fu style baguazhang. By this time, the train is "highballing" on a tortuous winding course, risking jumping the track at every tight turn. The centrifugal and centripetal forces generate power that cannot be dampened until the engine finally coasts into its home station as coolly and calmly as when it left (movements 83-108).

Returning to the Source

Sixiangquan is a "dance of energy." It has no boundaries, no limits. At the first level, it teaches us to appreciate the distinctions among the four internal arts in a single dance of changing energies and rhythms. In the next level, we sense the blend of these distinct energies, allowing them to become one, like a ribbon fluttering with the changing direction of a gusting and subsiding breeze. At still another level, we realize within ourselves that primordial natural process of yang with all of its qualities and quantities transforming to yin, and yin with all of its subtleties passing to yang. There are no preconceptions. It happens naturally and we follow. Sometimes we are the center moving out; sometimes we come from the eight directions, moving in. There are several levels before we reach an ultimate level, each one requiring observation, calculation, prediction, and much reflection. There is a level of the dance that would seem to open the spiritual gate and allow us to return to the "Great Ultimate," "the Taiji," and help us grasp a time and space before all movement. It becomes "meditation in motion"— total awareness.

And what of Wuji, a state so pristine that there is no place to enter and no need to issue forth, a state so full as to be empty, having nothing to grasp onto, an awareness so complete it is totally unaware? This may be too ethereal for our rational mind to contemplate, but for our spirit it is the journey home.

Victor Fu in Fu style taiji "repulse monkey"

(No one said it was easy!)

The Masters

The previous generation of masters such as Fu Yonghui, who have been most responsible for refining those arts passed on to us, was made up of people with vision of great philosophical depth. These arts were never merely physical expressions of their ego-seeking fame, nor were they merely fighters seeking the enemy's destruction. They were sensitive to their spiritual roots and to the practical applications of these philosophical values in their daily experience. By studying the natural world, they were, of course, also researching humankind's place in nature. Their arts were not solely fighting techniques nor performance forms. Rather, they were vehicles for understanding human behavior, knowledge of which could be used to take a life or save a life; there was no part of human endeavor where the principles they observed and practiced could not be applied. Their arts were metaphors for human behavior under the stress of daily life. The "enemy" could be conceived of at any level, physical, mental, emotional, and/or spiritual. If nature was a balancing act, then how much more so the human psyche? These arts served as physical healing, psychological therapy, philosophical inquiry, and even as spiritual reflection. As Mark Saito Senior, Master of Shorinjin Ryu Saito Ninjitsu, put it: "They (the dances) are silent prayers to my inner soul" (Phelps, 1997: 102). It is true then,

> Man follows the Earth. Earth follows Heaven.
> Heaven follows the Dao.
> Dao follows what is natural.
> – Feng & English, 1972: #25

In this context, the Fu family system of martial arts makes all the more sense. Therefore, the intense study and research of the Sixiang was not a luxury but a necessity.

Nevertheless, the art of sixiangquan is quite rare today. There are those who know the movements, however, there are only two masters who are qualified to teach it with any real depth to a Western audience. Even so, much is still missed. Mark Bow Sim, whose own mastery of the Fu system includes sixiangquan, has taught the form in the past but has not taught the whole form for several years now. She is well aware of its subtleties and in private conversations has helped me to understand the "treasures" hidden within the movements. Fu Shenglong, now living in Vancouver, Canada, will teach the form but has yet to pass the essence of the art to anyone. Fortunately, Victor is committed to expanding the Fu system internationally, which has inspired him to begin teaching this essence. No one else who has the form comes close to these two in technical skill nor in understanding what treasures are available within the art. Yet, the treasures are there for those who have the diligence to seek them out.

These arts are not lost. What is missing is the time, effort, and commitment to master them. Too many modern exponents have been satisfied to memorize movements and imitate mastery in the rush to seek recognition and acclaim. The true arts are not ladders to fame but teachers of the fundamental principles of life. They are vehicles through which to investigate and reflect on the balance between human behavior and natural laws—this Way offers long life; if not long life, then victory; if not victory, then peace of mind in the face of every challenge.

Notes

1 Since they lived in Guangzhou (Canton), Fu Yonghui and his family used the Cantonese pronunciation of his name, Fu Wing Fei. However, Mandarin is the official dialect of the People's Republic of China and the *Journal of Asian Martial Arts* uses their Pinyin Romanization system for all Chinese names.

2 The lead in to the news article is interesting. The editor's note indicates that despite his fame, they are concerned about him since they haven't heard anything about him in recent years. The editor then writes: "To find out what is going on with Mr. Fu, we sent out one of our journalists thousands of miles. . . ." (Zhai, n.d.).

3 Zou Yan was a younger contemporary of Aristotle (384-322 BCE). He was an early synthesizer of the myriad ancient shamanic practices of the Xia and Shang periods that slowly evolved into that which influenced Naturalist, Daoist and Confucian cosmologies.

4 Plotinus wrote: "The One [which we should equate with the Chinese term Wuji rather than with Taiji] is an Absolute, transcending all thought and is even beyond Being" (O'Meara, 1993: 55).

5 Not counting repetitions, e.g., three "parting wild horse's manes" equals one movement.

References

Einstein, A. (1950). *Out of my later years*. New York: Philosophical Library, Inc.

Feng, G. and English, J. (Trans.). (1972). *Lao Tsu: Tao te ching*. New York: Vintage Books.

Fu, Y. (1984 September). Newsletter of the Wudang Boxing Research Institute of the Guangzhou Martial Arts Association. Guangzhou: Guangzhou Martial Arts Association.

Henricks, R. (Trans.). (1989). *Lao-tzu–te-tao ching*. New York: Ballantine Books.

O'Meara, D. (1993). *Plotinus: An introduction to the Enneads*. Oxford: Clarendon Press.

Phelps, S. (1997). *Demon chaser: Five mountain path of the warrior spirit*. San Diego: Temple Bell, Ltd.

Phelps, S. (1996). The unique legacy of wudang master Fu Zhensong. *Journal of Asian Martial Arts*, 5(2): 90-105.

Watson, B. (Trans.). (1968). *The complete works of Chuang Tzu*. New York: Columbia University Press.

Zhai, R. (n.d.) *Fu Zhensong*. Guangzhou, China. Unpublished manuscript. Translated by Shannon K. Phelps.

Internal Martial Arts of Taiwan:
An Interview with Marcus Brinkman

by Kevin Craig, M.A.

Photograph courtesy of Dr. Mark Griffin.

Robert Smith's classic book, *Chinese Boxing: Masters and Methods* (1974), was an inspiration for many martial artists of my generation and the first introduction many of us had to the *neijia* (internal) arts. His vivid descriptions of his encounters with accomplished martial artist during his years on Taiwan fired our imaginations and launched many a quest that will last a lifetime.

Smith's first teacher on Taiwan, and the one he returned to throughout his time there, was Hong Yixiang. Smith tells of his xingyiquan practice with Hong as well as his meetings with Hong's teacher, Zhang Junfeng, and Hong Yixiang's brother, Hong Yimian. Of the many things that Smith says of Hong perhaps the most telling is his final remark: "... I cannot imagine a better ally to have if things tended toward the physical" (Smith, 1990: 10).

When he moved to Taiwan in 1985, Marcus Brinkman was one of the many Americans to pick up the story of the neijia arts on Taiwan some twenty-six years after Smith began his journey there. During his ten years on the island, Marcus and a small group of expatriate foreigners were among Hong Yixiang's last students. After his time with Hong, and during his final five years on Taiwan, Marcus extensively studied baguazhang with Luo Dexiu, one of Hong's senior students. Luo is living proof of

Smith's observation that Hong exemplified the principle that the job of the teacher is to teach the student how to learn and find out facts for themselves. Luo has continued his extensive research into baguazhang theory and practice throughout Taiwan and China and had developed into one of the best known exponents of the art in the world today.

Following is an interview with Marcus Brinkman, OMD, senior baguazhang student of Luo Dexiu. In it he relates many of the unique insights and experiences he had during his extensive study with his teachers Luo Dexiu and Hong Yixiang.

Group photo of Hong's xingyiquan class, dated August 13, 1988.
Photograph courtesy of M. Binkman.

- **Robert Smith wrote *Chinese Boxing* in the fifties [Smith arrived in Taipei in August 1959]. You visited Taiwan almost thirty years later. Did Hong Yixiang resemble the character portrayed in Smith's book?**

Well, in those thirty years, much of Hong's bar-brawler traits receded while the gentleman-scholar aspect of his complex personality moved to the fore. When I met Hong, his house and teaching space were hidden within the maze of allies in old Taipei. A worn out, barely decipherable shingle hung above his little medical office advertising his martial arts school and Chinese medical practice. Hong claimed to be in retirement when I began training with him. As far as I know, besides our small xingyiquan class of about eight or nine, his only other teaching obligations were his crack-of-dawn qigong classes. He was also still active as the head official of Taiwan's martial arts association.

- **Can you describe Hong Yixiang?**

Hong's physical appearance was quite intimidating. His body was massive. Although he only stood about five foot nine, the girth of his legs, hips, arms, neck, shoulders, and abdomen were extreme. His voice sounded rather hoarse and gravelly and when he spoke Mandarin it was often punctuated with spicy Taiwanese slang. Overall, he was a remarkable character.

• **What was your primary course of study with Hong?**

Xingyiquan. Occasionally, however, we would change directions for a month or two and practice White Crane [*Bai He*], taijiquan, or qigong.

• **Were Hong's martial skills as formidable as reputed to be?**

Yes. Hong's inside fighting skills were very well developed. His movements were relaxed and natural. Even in his mid-sixties, his sensitivity and power were well maintained. For a man his size, he possessed amazing body integration. His ability to either isolate or unify the various muscle groups of his body was quite impressive. In playful moods he would sometimes demonstrate his unique abdominal control, leisurely lifting, dropping, and rolling his hefty center. He could suddenly propel himself forward with a powerful spinal wave, advancing his huge mass to a distant point without losing body alignment. This showcased his agile weight shifts and accentuated his drawing and releasing skills.

• **Hong's power has been well documented, but what about his sensitivity and grappling skills?**

Hong's brutish physical appearance didn't prepare you for his acute listening skills [*tingjing*]. His hand and finger dexterity were exceptional and greatly embellished his employment of sticking, adhering, connecting, and following. Partly due to his masterful grappling skills, and partly due to his ability to integrate his large mass, Hong was an exceptional martial artist.

Hong Yixiang officiating at a tournament in Taipei, circa 1986-87.
Photograph courtesy of Christopher Bates.

• **Could you elaborate in regard to his sticking [*zhan*] and adhering [*nian*] skills?**

Hong's sticking and adhering skills were unlike anything I had previously seen. Upon contact, he was able to grab the skin and use it as a body handle. This kind of body handle affords exceptional control over an opponent. The underlying fascia, which weaves into the supporting skeletal frame, may be accessed with a flesh entwining hand maneuver similar to that used by Chinese bonesetters and masseurs. The entwining begins with a vigorous rub which quickly changes to a tight winding up of any excess, loose flesh. Hong would use this as a set up, and, in mid-course change the skin handle to a short, open-handed palm strike. Just as easily he would lead his victims to and fro, paralyzed in his grip. He was able to grasp the flesh on most any part of the human anatomy, including under the arms, around the chest and even on the face and cheeks. He claimed to be able to tear the flesh in this fashion, and, though I never witnessed such, I believe he possessed the power to do so.

• **What other martial attributes were you impressed with while training with Hong?**

Hong was able to produce barely visible ripples or large, undulating waves throughout his substantial frame. His precise integration of and control over his body embellished his use of *suai shou* (whipping palm). As a method of making contact he could apply whipping with just his fingers, inflicting stinging welts over the body's surface. As a maiming assaultive maneuver, he could unify his mass with enough force to break bones and rupture organs. In teaching, he stressed a smooth entrainment of movement starting from the ground, routing into the extremities and issuing through strategic junctures on the arms, hands, or fingertips. In training, he stressed versatility of this skill and taught many of its alternate uses and modes of power.

• **What are some common martial applications of whipping?**

Taijiquan, baguazhang, and xingyiquan all utilize whipping. While this *jing* is common to all three, its *xing* and *yi* [shape and mind] may be altered according to a variety of circumstances. The dimensions of the wave within whipping palm may vary in size, symmetry, and tempo; while the quality of mind directed through its length may vary according to usage. For instance, whipping is sometimes used from a distance, as if throwing a large net. In this case, its wave starts out as large and circular but, at the end of its projection, hooks inward sharply. Whipping may be short and stinging or large and engulfing. Upon contact the power can change instantly from hard and immobile to soft and supple. With the addition of rotation throughout the arm, whipping becomes a variation of rise, fall, and overturn. Whipping can be combined with shaking, coiling, turning over, adhering, sticking, connecting, following, etc. It is suitable for either short or long jing releases and allows good control after impact, hence its adaptability as a grappling tool.

• **I attended a Luo Dexiu seminar recently at which Luo talked about the energetic effects of various strikes. Can you comment on the effect of whipping palm?**

Luo often discussed energetic effect within the genre of traditional terms: *jing, qi,* and *shen*. Both transmission of power and the reaction of the object effected by that transmission have a fundamental relationship to jing, qi, and shen. Within an internal art, health cultivation context, the constituent components of power transmission, xing, and yi are considered byproducts of the core energetic elements jing, qi, and shen; while within the context of martial cultivation, xing and yi are constituents devoted to the assault and disarrangement of jing, qi, and shen. Luo trains students to interpret energetic effect in relation to both of these perspectives. Weighing the energetic effects of an outside influence is partly a matter of understanding the energetic nature of the object receiving the influence.

This single palm change opens with forceful, rising, whipping palm to the opponents's flank (A-1 to A-2). Marcus (wearing the white shirt) positions his back leg to allow for a spacious, dropping rollback (A-3). This opens up the opponent's tight on-guard stance. As the opponent loses his balance slightly, Marcus closes the gap (A-4), changing direction of his attack to the inside (A-5), wrapping around his opponent's neck, preparing for a take-down or throw (A-6).

Using his right hand, Marcus deflects the opponent's right hand away from his centerline (B-1 and B2). As the opponent attempts to defend his center (B-3), Marcus moves in to tie-up the opponent's hands (B-4), isolating the arms and "wraps" outward to secure an armlock which flows into a throw (B-5 & B-6).

Special thanks to Aarvo for helping with the technical section.

- So, Luo teaches that both the bio-energetic properties of the body and the matter-energy properties of power development are taken into account?

Yes. Xing and yi are terms which correspond to the internal art's matter-energy properties of power development. Jing, qi, and shen are terms which correspond to the traditional Chinese medical view of the body's bio-energetic properties. In martial terms, some kinds of power are relatively more useful in disturbing [one's) shen. Other kinds of power are directed towards causing disruption of jing. In actuality, because both jing and shen are representations of qi [unified and separated states of qi, respectively], the body's normal qi circulation will be affected in either case. The qi may constrict, causing rigidity. The qi may disperse, leading to inability to respond. The qi may float upward causing a loss of stability or it may sink downward causing double-weightedness.

Learning to cultivate the numerous variables of xing and yi promotes an understanding of the transmission half of energetic effect. The other half may be explained as response and requires some knowledge of the nature of qi and *xue* [blood] from a Chinese medical perspective. Understanding the body's response to a variety of common stimuli can assist in selecting the right power for each individual encounter. If an opponent has spent many years developing a special skill, such as iron body or *song*, it is important to understand the best way to disturb their particular expression of jing, qi, and shen.

- This seems to relate somewhat to bagua's *tanjing* [testing skill]?

Yes, in a sense. Testing or researching [*tan*] is a method of evaluating your opponent. This often refers to an attack used to create a specific response or to evaluate an opponent's reaction to a threat. It enhances your comprehension of his strengths and weaknesses. This method of evaluation can range from being relatively gross to being quite refined. For instance, Hong Yixiang often employed a testing tactic referred to as *jia jia zhen zhen* [fake fake real real]. The concept behind this ploy is to test an opponent's reactions with full power attacks. These attacks are intended to break an opponent's yi, disconcerting his ability to respond in a precise manner. The diversionary aspect of this ploy is the fake, while delivery with full power is the real. Jia jia zhen zhen is a very concrete example of testing. More sophisticated methods of testing are initiated before physical contact is initiated. The subtler applications of testing share common features with some of the diagnostic arts of Chinese medicine.

- What are some common features?

Well, the Chinese penchant of refining a skill to an almost imperceptible degree of complexity applies to testing in much the same way it applies to skills used by qigong and Chinese medical doctors. It involves evaluating features of the body which correspond to an opponent's degree of physical and neural integration. It's actually quite amazing what can be revealed about the inside by observing the outside. Essentially, this skill comes back to evaluating one's jing, qi, and shen.

- Is it true that Hong's martial demonstrations were often brutal?

Yes, but I never saw anyone suffer any serious injury. Students, however, often felt the need for a spinal adjustment after one of Hong's demos, which Hong himself would usually provide. *Pai da*, patting of the body, and *nie*, plucking of the flesh and tendons under the scapulae or hidden deep within the armpits, would send fleeting shocks along the nerve branches. After a few of these treatments, just the thought of Hong's prodding hands had the power to revive you. Hong was a Chinese doctor specialized in *die da sun shang* [trauma or hit medicine], so he was a great person to have around if there was an occasional injury. He used a lot of massage and bone-setting techniques. I believe those skills also embellished his impressive power and grappling skills as well.

- **What was Hong's training regimen like?**

A big part of Hong's training regimen was *zhanzhuang* [standing meditation]. He pushed us to stand in *santi shi* well beyond the burning phase, As Hong pushed our limits during these standing sessions, I secretly wondered why I would pay someone to torture me. In time, however, I began to look forward to this labor. My overall health seemed to improve, my mind seemed sharper, and my body felt stronger. Gradually, we integrated static postures from xingyi's metal fist [pi quan] into our standing. Hong stressed long body and deep stances while holding these postures. He also insisted upon an extreme corkscrewing momentum within them, such that the body could find no resting place. Holding these extended postures challenged the will [zhi]. Simultaneously, from the corkscrewing movement, drilling began to emerge. Eventually the postures became smoothly integrated until drilling revealed the natural rise, fall, and overturn of pi quan.

- **What specific postural alignments did Hong address in teaching santi shi?**

Chicken foot serves as a reminder to keep the weight on the back leg. Dragon waist serves as a reminder to feel for the true rotation of the waist. This prevents arching at the lower back hinge and helps to unify the upper and lower halves of the body. Bear shoulders serve as a reminder to keep correct tension through the scapular region of the back. This connects the arms through the back and shoulders while closing the chest's centerline. And tiger neck serves as a reminder to eliminate the cervical arching and to extend through the crown point. This slightly tractions the spine from above.

Practically speaking, these postural alignments naturally adjust the body in relation to the "three external harmonies" (*wai san he*): coordination of wrist/ankle, elbow/knee, and shoulder/waist. Hong also paid particular attention to the nuances of the hand shape.

- **In what way?**

Hong became increasingly concerned with making minute corrections in hand shape. Many people are familiar with adjusting the tension between the thumb and forefinger. This region, the "tiger's mouth," is considered a collection depot where the body's "upper sea of qi" may be accessed. He would occasionally palpate this area to evaluate the strength of a student's or patient's pulmonary and respiratory functions [upper sea of qi]. Hong extended this theory to include tension between the thumb and the third, fourth and fifth fingers as well. In this way, the yi begins to spread evenly throughout the hand and promotes a thawing sensation throughout the forearm, shoulder, and gradually into the back. At this stage, the hand is better able to shape itself around the hollow in the middle of the palm [lao gong]. The hand, like other bodily terrains, is seen to represent a microcosm of the body. Attention to the hand's shape can indirectly affect the structure of the body and clarity of the mind.

• **What is the significance of creating a hollow around lao gong?**
The minute alignments of the hand and fingers around lao gong constitute a subtle neural integration technique. The center of the palm corresponds to the heart and is intimately related to the brain and nervous system. The fingers are said to communicate directly [via the meridian network] with the nervous system's sense organs. According to the principles of xingyiquan, form gives shape to mind and mind leads qi.

Left: Luo Dexiu in standing post posture (*zhanzhuang*).
Right: in xingyiquan dragon posture. *Photographs courtesy of* M. *Brinkman*.

• **I've heard former students of Hong claim that his xingyi possessed a definite baguazhang flavor.**
Unbeknownst to most of Hong's xingyi students, Hong's pi quan [metal chopping fist] is a linear version of baguazhang's single palm change.

• **What do you mean?**
Well, although single palm change expresses drilling, rising, falling, and overturning, it is generally considered to demonstrate a horizontal circle [heng jing]. The pi quan of Hong's xingyi system also emphasizes rising, falling, and overturning, but it primarily expresses a vertical circle [shu jing]. It uses a rising body wave carried up through the spine and coordinated with a half step [ban bu]. Of these two single palm changes, one is considered the post-heaven [houtian] version, while the other is the pre-heaven [qiantian] version. The first is considered a circle on a line, while the second is a circle on a circle. Most importantly, both single palm changes entrain an ascending and descending spinal wave in coordination with central torso rotation. The former emphasizes more rising and

falling while the latter emphasizes rotation around the vertical axis. The half step is also considered a post-heaven method of maintaining unity while in motion. Continuous *kou/bai* stepping implies a higher order of pre-heaven power development.

• **I've heard that Hong had developed "dragon body." What does this mean?**

The characteristic spinal waves associated with *wu lung bai wei* [black dragon shakes its tail] possess a spiraling or serpentine quality. Wu lung bai wei integrates the larger spirals of bagua's mother palms into one essential action, *chan si* [reeling silk]. The spiraling of the eight mother palms generally appears in larger configurations. Within wu lung bai wei, however, the spiraling is accentuated through the trunk and is rather compact. Hence its undulating, dragon body appearance.

• **What internal cultivation concepts are involved in "dragon body'" training?**

It links the inside and outside of the body, so that movement is both internally and externally circular. Conceptually, this involves jings known as *chan si jing* [reeling silk skill] and chou si jing [drawing silk skill]. The two represent a dialectic relationship of external and internal. In this context, drawing silk is the internal component.

• **Did Hong introduce "bone marrow washing" [*xi xue jing*] to his students?**

Indirectly, yes. His methods, however, were generally oriented towards fundamental principles. I would characterize Hong's training methods as the post-heaven aspect of bone marrow washing. This aspect deals largely with reparation and strengthening of the physical body as well as essential movement patterns and principles. Hong's idea of achieving this involved routine standing sessions and repetitious practice of xingyi's *wuxing quan* [five-element fist]. For myself, I endured Hong's post-heaven training but later sought the expertise of Luo Dexiu in regard to understanding the principles of "pre-heaven" baguazhang.

• **Can you briefly describe that aspect of your studies with Luo?**

Pre-heaven baguazhang, like *xi xue jing*, is initially concerned with curbing excess energy expenditure of the nervous system. For instance, immoderation of the emotions is seen to tax the nervous system, and, consequently deplete the jing [the body's material basis/ including endocrine secretions]. As one learns to curb excessive energy expenditures, this process is refined. The mind seeks to quell energy expenditures at their inception and recycle energy before there is much loss. While energy conservation is the initial aim, advanced methods strongly stimulate the nervous system to fuel endocrine secretion. Practitioners learn to funnel this rarefied substance back to the nervous system to replenish bodily substances such as marrow, spinal fluid, and brain matter. *Qiantian* baguazhang is intended to reintegrate the nervous system towards a higher order of function and purpose. Luo cautioned that concentrated training in this area requires an environment suited to the special needs of the practitioner. Qiantian baguazhang has a strong influence upon brain and body development. Its cultivation may exacerbate existing physical and emotional imbalances or create imbalances when lacking a guided regimen and/or practiced according to erroneous guidelines. This is invariably so for martial artists who are driven by their desire for greater power. In advanced stages of cultivation, xi xue jing is touted to actually bring about a metamorphosis of the physical body. In men, the penis is said to retract inward while the cranium becomes enlarged. These manifestations, however, are not necessarily within the focus of martial practices.

- **Does the bone marrow washing aspect of pre-heaven baguazhang have any direct connection to martial skills?**

Yes. A great deal of connection, especially if you consider the nervous system's role in the development of agility [*mingjue*] and power [*gongli*]. *Shougong* [collection practice] is the aspect of qiantian baguazhang involved with redirecting bio-energy back to its source, regenerating the material basis of the nervous system [*jingqi*]. In theory, extending the mind's sensitivity inward puts the nervous system in contact with the material body [*jing*]. In martial practices such as *sanshou*, *roushou*, and *tuishou*, developing this kind of sensitivity is fundamental to cultivation of good tactile listening skills [*tingjing*]. During shougong, the mind is directed inward, while *ting* directs the mind outward towards the surface of the body. From a modern Chinese medical standpoint, tactile nerve branches near the skin surface derive nourishment from core neural substances such as marrow [brain and spinal cord]. Development of good *ting* skills are therefore partly dependent on the cultivation and reparation of these materials.

- **How does one transit from post-heaven to pre-heaven?**

As a didactic process, neijiaquan typically progresses from "mind-follows-body" to "body-follows-mind." This process is ordinarily suggestive of methods which link the body and mind along their common neural pathways. Luo often substituted the terms sensitivity and sensation for the terms mind and body, respectively. Cultivation of mind is analogous to cultivation of sensitivity, likewise, cultivation of body is analogous to cultivation of sensation. When sensation becomes abundant the mind is better able to feel its movement, hence "body-follows-mind." As the mind becomes increasingly attuned to body sensation it may begin to coordinate with its movement. Luo referred to this as the "mind-feel-ing-itself." As awareness of the body's frequency becomes clear, one becomes increasingly able to integrate external body movement around this frequency.

- **So this dichotomy of "mind-follows-body" and "body-follows-mind" depicts a post-heaven to pre-heaven transformation?**

Yes. A rudimentary explanation of jing, qi, and shen is conveyed in the *Yijing's* [*Book of Changes*] three-tiered heaven, human, and earth trigram. This symbol is more immediately expressive of the dichotomy of unity and separation implicit within the three treasures: jing, qi, shen. In this context, jing and shen may be understood as gradations of qi. Representing unity, earth and jing are both perceived as relatively heavy and still manifestations of qi. Representing separation, heaven and shen are perceived as relatively light and moving manifestations of qi. These models are only two of many models which convey identical energetic circumstances within a sundry of contextual settings.

146

The attacker strikes with a forward jab which Marcus diverts downward (C-1 and C-2), then immediately whips to the opponent's center (C-3). This maneuver engages the opponent's defenses (C-4). In this case, Marcus wraps around the back of the opponent's neck (C-5) while using the opponent's right arm for additional leverage (C-6 and C-7).

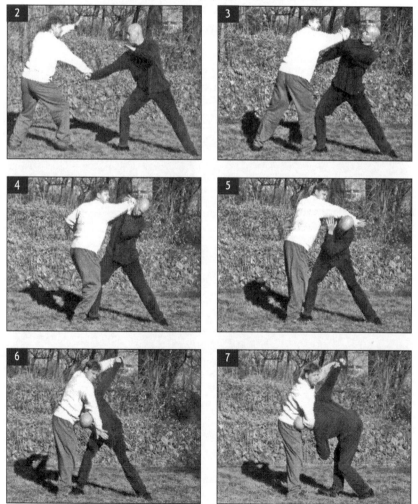

• What about the intermediate positions of "human" and qi?

Heaven, human, and earth may be perceived as either a sequential series of transformations or as a synergistic transformation. *Yijing* theory deems this process from simple to complex and from complex to simple. In other words, from unity to separation and separation to unity. In separation [complexity], we refer to its sequential arrangement; while in unity [simplicity], we refer to its synergistic construction. The synergistic construction may be likened to viewing stereograms, in which case the visual senses are engaged. A three-dimensional image appears as one bifurcates the visual focal point. Initially, one tends either to over-focus or under-focus the eyes. The image tends to shift between a single, focused image and a split, unfocused image. The trick is to find an intermediate kind of focus. When this is achieved, two dimensions merge to create a unified third dimension. These circumstances are analogous to the intermediate focus required to harmonize the *san bao* [the three treasures]: jing, qi, and shen. In practice, maintaining precise harmonization is synonymous with drawing silk skill. The two dimensions, jing and shen, unify as a third dimension, qi.

• You said, "in which case the visual senses are engaged." How does this apply to the body-mind dichotomy?

Production of this phenomenon may be initiated by separating the attention equally between the left and right palm surfaces. Attention is then slowly guided away from the palms surfaces into the space between the palms. The body begins to react to a sense of separation or unification as the mind shifts from the palm surfaces to the space between the palms. Although tactile sensitivity is focused upon the ends of the separate nerve branches, integration is ultimately aimed at their source, the left and right halves of the brain. As the ability to focus upon these subtle sensations increases, so does the possibility of organizing the structure and movement patterns around these sensations. At this level, coordination of the outside with the inside is actuated.

Marcus in baquazhang posture "point to the sky, mark the earth."
Photograph courtesy of M. Binkman.

Marcus and Luo in a two-person baguazhang practice.
Photograph courtesy of M. Binkman.

• **Can you talk about Luo's approach to teaching qigong and internal martial arts?**

Luo emphasizes a how-to-train approach to his teaching. He is very clear about teaching process. His methodical and mechanical approach to training the body reflects his earlier training period with representatives of Gao Style baguazhang, while his approach in training the mind reflect his latter training period with Liu Qian of the Sun Xikun lineage. He suggests that whether one is practicing the body, the mind, or a combination of the two [qi], one should clearly distinguish each. Ultimately, there is a merging of these methods, but first one must understand how to isolate and identify these aspects during practice. In this capacity we started circle-walking practice right away. He suggested however that I simultaneously learn Eight Brocades qigong, and some various standing practices as well.

• **Why did Luo begin with the Eight Brocades?**

Like other systems of qigong, the Brocades are touted as a mind/body integration method. Some systems of qigong emphasize more body. Others, emphasize more mind. They are also differentiated according to purpose, ego medical, longevity, martial, etc. The Eight Brocades are fairly generic in their approach. They lay a foundation of principles, which can be applied with emphasis upon either *jing* or *yi*. Luo began using the Eight Brocades to help students identify the principles inherent in the majority of neijiaquan practices. For instance the energetic relationship of *kan* [water] and *li* [fire] as a key in understanding the relationship between the body's central nervous system and glandular systems. Luo teaches that reparation of these systems is necessary in preparing the body for internal martial arts training. Working with the Eight Brocades is also a good way to begin exercising the basic vocabulary needed to discuss qigong and internal martial arts practice in general. I would consider it a good intermediate style of qigong.

• **Could you elaborate a bit in regard to training aspects emphasized by Luo?**

Pre-heaven baguazhang begins with basic circle-walking practice. Circle-walking is considered a type of moving practice [*dong gong*], while *zhanzhuang*, or standing practice, is considered a kind of stillness practice [*jing gong*]. Luo often begins students with moving gong as he considers it suitable for the beginner's nervous system. Some movement is seen to harmonize better with a beginner's frequency. At this stage, Luo observed that the mind may resist being forced into immediate stillness. Forcing a student into stillness too quickly can exacerbate existing imbalances.

- **Do you think it is necessary to understand so much about the medical relationships of internal arts training?**

Historically, China's internal cultivation and medical traditions do not lie far apart. This points out the necessity of having some expertise in both subjects. Lately, there has been increased awareness centering around unqualified teachers of neijia arts. Although these charges have ordinarily been made in regard to bogus internal strength practices, it is equally important to find teachers who are aware of potential health risk. Martial artist are often the worst offenders in this area. Unnatural extremes applied in order to achieve greater powers of mind or body may comes with a price.

Pinyin	Wade-Giles	
ban bu	pan pu	半步
chou si jing	ch'ou ssu ch'ing	抽絲勁
guo shu	kuo shu	國術
heng jing	heng ch'ing	橫勁
hou tian	hou t'ien	後天
lao gong	lao kung	勞宮
nei san he	nei san ho	內三合
nie	nieh	捏
pai	p'ai	拍
san bao	san pao	三寶
shou gong	shou kung	收功
shu jing	shu ch'ing	豎勁
shuai shou	shuai shou	摔手
tan	t'an	探
wai san he	wai san ho	外三合
wu long bai wei	wu lung pai wei	烏龍擺尾
xi sui jin	hsi sui ch'in	洗髓勁
xian tian	hsien t'ien	先天
yi	i	意
zhi	chih	志

Reference

Smith, R. (1990). *Chinese boxing: Masters and methods.* Berkeley, CA: North Atlantic Books.

chapter 12

Throwing Techniques
in the Internal Martial Arts
An Elucidation of the Guiding Principle
of "Sticking and Following"

by Tim Cartmell, B.A.

Jake Burroughs, left, and the author practicing techniques
using the principles of sticking and following.
All photographs by Dana Benjamin.

Introduction

One could argue that throws are throws, no matter the style. All throws and takedowns are executed in fundamentally the same way. Excepting minor details in method, this assertion is true: there are only so many ways to put an opponent on the ground. All types of throws are based on leverage, manipulation of mass, removal of support, and the use of momentum and gravity. There are, however some concrete differences in the ways throws are set up and executed in different styles. Among styles, the variation in throwing techniques is found in four broad areas: entries, grips, body method, and strategy of application. The Chinese Internal Styles have unique variations of common throws, based on a unique strategy of application.

Entries will primarily be determined by the ability or desirability of using striking techniques, the types of throws preferred, and the relative positioning of the fighters. The threat of strikes, type of clothing, uniform or lack thereof, and types of throws to be applied will be the primary determinate of the grips. The presence of weapons will also greatly influence the above variables, but we will limit this discussion to unarmed fighting. The thrower's body method (here we are most concerned with the methods of generating force, including mobility in footwork, level change, types of power and particular use of rhythm) will also greatly influence the types of throws used. Finally, the chosen strategy of application will have the greatest influence on throwing methods, including the types of entries and grips used, as well as the methods of generating force.

This chapter is concerned with the throws used in the three most popular styles of Chinese Internal Martial Arts (CIMA), xingyiquan, baguazhang, and taijiquan. The throws used in the CIMA are similar to comparable throws found in other styles and are heavily influenced by *shuaijiao* (Chinese wrestling). What makes the throwing methods of the CIMA styles unique is their emphasis on the principle of "sticking and following." In reality, sticking and following can be viewed as the underlying strategy of the entire throwing method of all three internal styles, and is therefore the strongest influence on the entries, grips and body method used.

Sticking and Following

The name "sticking and following" (*zhannian/liansui*) is used to describe a united strategic concept of technical application in the CIMA. Although most often associated with the various arts of taijiquan, the principle applies to the other internal styles as well. A central tenet of the internal styles is the avoidance of the use of force directly against a stronger force. The corollary to this tenet is the concept of "borrowing force," that is, using an attacker's force to one's advantage. The means of borrowing an opponent's force is realized within the skills of sticking and following. The stick and follow skill set is so important the CIMA have evolved a number of specific training exercises designed exclusively to foster the skill (variations of the popular "push hands" practice being the most recognizable). The concept of sticking and following evolved from the most basic paradox of personal combat, how to develop a method that allows a smaller and weaker man to defeat a heavier and stronger opponent.

Let's go into the definition of the terms "stick" and "follow" as they apply to the CIMA. "Sticking" implies a consistency of contact, and by extension, contact from which the opponent cannot escape. Imagine fly paper stuck to your hand that passively thwarts all effort to shake it off. Or for a more universal image, imagine walking in a pool. No matter the direction you move, the water yields to your advance without losing contact while following your advance without the slightest gap in pressure. It is impossible to escape the ubiquitous and constant contact pressure of the water, yet the nature of the water is "passive." Similarly, the internal fighter's contact with his opponent is "passive" in the sense of non-opposition of the opponent's force. To "stick" is not the same as to resist. The constant adherence to the opponent is made active when the concept of "following" is included as well. Although the internal fighter seeks to maintain constant contact without opposition of force, he must also actively follow the opponent to maintain contact while seeking the most advantageous position.

Another way of understanding sticking and following is through the idea of "filling in the gaps." Wherever there is space, the internal fighter enters to fill the gap. A very important part of filling in the gaps is the amount of surface area covered. In general, the more surface area one is able to contact, the more control and potential for power one will have. For example, you would have exponentially more control over an opponent if you wrapped your arms around him and pulled him tightly against you in a body lock (bear hug) as opposed to holding his wrist with your fingertips at arm's length. In most cases, the more surface area of your body in contact with the opponent (from a superior position) the more control you will have, the less effort you will need to effect your technique, and the less likely your opponent will be able to escape or counter.

Finally, it is very important to realize sticking and following can and should be done with any and all parts of your body. Not only the arms and legs, but all parts of the torso and even the head can be used to maintain contact, control the opponent and issue force where appropriate. Many times potentially successful throws are thwarted by a lack of committed contact or gaps in pressure. Space you are not controlling is space your opponent can use to escape.

Entries

Obviously, it is impossible to throw an opponent without making contact, and contrary to striking techniques, contact must be of a continuous duration at least until the throw is completed. How best to make contact and set up the throw is the subject of entries. Entering into and setting up a technique will be determined by several variables, including the combination of throws with striking techniques, the particular set of techniques to be applied, and opportunities based on the combatants reactions and relative positions. Leaving aside sport fights with specific rules, entering into a throw in an actual fight will have as a primary consideration the safety of the fighter as he enters. For the purposes of this chapter, we'll assume the CIMA fighter is facing a ready and capable opponent, face on, in a hands up fight.

In general, all-in fights will begin with blows before the fighters close to grappling range. Although many confrontations start with attempts at grabbing, or begin from extreme close range before strikes are thrown, being struck is always a concern at any range. The strategic preference for the CIMA styles is close range. It is important to note that being at close range doesn't preclude striking, but will always include wrestling. The internal fighter not only wants to get close, he wants to get close and obtain a superior position as efficiently as possible ("superior positions" are those which provide a great margin of safety from blows, and allow one to apply most or all of one's body power with superior leverage). At its most basic level, this involves avoiding being stuck or ending up in an inferior position.

From the point of view of a fighter, fights will start in one of two ways; either you will take the offensive and attack first, or your opponent will attack first and you will react defensively. There is a popular stereotypical idea that internal styles are "soft" and internal stylists prefer to wait passively while an opponent attacks first in order to take advantage of his force. This is not true. While it is absolutely necessary to learn how to deal with incoming aggressive force while reacting defensively, this is not preferred. The preferred strategy of entry is to attack first, causing the opponent to react and then using his reaction to one's own advantage. The fighter who acts and continues to act maintains an advantage over the fighter who is forced to continually react. One simply cannot win a fight while on defense.

With our strategy of preemptive attack in mind, let's look at the specifics of entries. Because of the threat of blows, the internal fighter in general will not simply charge directly in to obtain grips. Rushing in towards a ready opponent leaves one too vulnerable to being struck. Even the popular and effective strike high, level change and shoot for the legs strategy popular in MMA is not seen in CIMA entries. Again, the threat of being struck (or cut if the opponent is armed) disallows this type of entry from the CIMA repertoire. When facing an opponent hands up and ready to fight, the CIMA fighter needs to make contact, control or clear the opponent's hands, and obtain contact in a superior position. In order to make first contact and force the opponent to react, the CIMA fighter prefers to attack with strikes or a combination of feints and strikes to elicit a response from the opponent, and will enter into a superior position as the situation allows. Another important point of strategy is that the CIMA fighter will seek to maintain continuous pressure and contact after initial contact is made, conforming to the master strategy of sticking and following.

Grips

The term "grips" is used here is the broad sense of contact with an opponent, and is not limited to grasping with the hands. The particular configuration of contact and the amount of control it affords will directly determine the particular throwing technique that is appropriate to the situation. Fights are dynamic, and points of contact will change as the fight goes on. The strategy of the CIMA fighter is to continually seek greater and greater control. Application of sticking and following is crucial to success in obtaining, maintaining and improving control. As mentioned above, the more surface area of one's body that is in contact with an opponent, in a superior position, the greater the degree of control over the opponent, and the less overall effort needed to apply a technique. The CIMA fighter will train to use all parts of his body to connect with and apply force to an opponent. One point of interest is that, in contrast to most Western styles of wrestling, CIMA techniques rarely include locking the hands together. Although locking one's hands together in a closed grip may provide a stronger static hold, the principle of sticking and following is better served with the hands free to move independently of one another.

From the instant of initial contact, the CIMA fighter seeks to maintain contact and pressure, while ever seeking to improve position and control. This calls for a type of "dynamic gripping" that allows the fighter to maintain contact pressure while not being stuck to a single place. The general flow of pressure is inward toward the opponent's center of gravity, and sometimes tangentially to turn or pull the opponent's center of gravity. The ultimate goal is control. Most CIMA throwing techniques will be completed from body-to-body contact, attempting to throw an opponent with wrist or elbow control alone is seen comparatively less (it should be noted that joint locking techniques (*qinna*) applied to the extremities will often result in a fall, but this is a secondary effect of their primary purpose of breaking or dislocating a joint).

Body Method

All types of martial arts have evolved specific methods of developing power. Without power, there is no "martial art." The particular way a martial artist develops and applies power is generally referred to as "body method" (*shen fa*). Body method will include the movements of the torso and limbs, displacement through space (including footwork and level change) and the rhythm of the body as a whole. The types of power developed are primarily determined by the strategy of application of technique. When creating methods of developing power, it is only logical to work backward from the goal to its means of completion. Since the goal of any martial discipline worthy of the moniker "art" is to impart a method that allows the weaker to defeat the stronger, the body method of the CIMA is, by necessity, based on the principle of sticking and following.

Most throws are very similar in terms of mechanics. For a specific throw to be executed efficiently, fulcrums must be placed in the correct place and power must be applied in the right direction. These fundamental conditions cannot be altered if the throw is to "work" in an efficient manner. How a fighter moves into position and how he develops power will differ however, and these differences in body method will show the most pronounced variance between the CIMA and other styles of martial art.

Let's take a more in-depth look at the body method of Chinese Internal Martial Arts. Although there is some variation in the methods of movement and force development, some principles of body movement remain constant among the various CIMA styles (these principles are not exclusive to CIMA however, and can be found in a number of other martial styles). First and foremost, all styles of CIMA place a heavy emphasis on developing "whole body power" (*zheng ti jing*). Whole body power refers to generating force with the strongest muscles of the body, radiating this force outward through the torso and extremities while each successive part of the body contributes to and magnifies the force until it is issued outward into the target. Inherent in the concept is the idea of using the weight of one's entire body mass as much as possible. The strongest muscles of the body, and the muscles primarily concerned with the initial and most powerful generation of force all have one end attached to the pelvis. Whole body power originates from there. In order to generate and magnify force from the center outward, force must move in a wave-like fashion. Since all points of a wave have force, any part of the body may be used to apply force to the opponent. This facet of the body method is very important to the CIMA fighter's ability to stick and follow his opponent with any part of his body. This is a clear example of the principle of sticking and following dictating the type of body method necessary to apply CIMA techniques successfully.

155

Strategy

As discussed above, in order to qualify as a martial "art" the guiding principle of development must be the creation of strategies and techniques that provide a method for the smaller and weaker fighter to overcome the larger and stronger. The first principle that emerges from this demand is the futility of opposing a stronger force directly with a weaker force. It is often said in regards to CIMA technique that one should never use "force against force." This is incorrect. Force will always be applied against some resistant force, even in the absence of conscious resistance on the part of an opponent, it will still be necessary to overcome the inherent resistance of the opponent's weight, no matter how mechanically efficient the technique. It should be properly stated that force should never be used directly against a greater force. If your own force is sufficient to overcome the resistant force of an opponent, your force can be efficiently applied, even if the opponent resists. Sticking to an opponent by its very nature requires that some level of force must be constantly applied, like water flowing downstream, not necessarily attempting to overcome the opponent's force yet not retreating from any level of resistance. The ultimate goal is the application of one's total whole body power toward a "dead angle" (*si jiao*), an angle from which the opponent cannot offer resistance.

This brings us to the next point; while sticking and following an opponent, what do we do when his resistant force becomes greater than our applied force? This study is found in the principle of "transformation." The overall goal is to borrow the opponent's force and transform it into our own force. This principle in application can be seen in various forms, from the "push when pulled/ pull when pushed" concept popular in many throwing arts to more subtle methods of unbalancing and controlling the opponent that are barely noticeable until it is too late for him to counter. In taijiquan, this concept is referred to as "no letting go and no resistance". Simply stated, when the opponent's resistant force threatens to overcome your sticking force and cause you to become resistant to the point of rigidity, you yield to the force without disjoining at that specific point of contact. Conversely all other points of contact (or potential contact) continue to pressure in toward the opponent's center, ever seeking greater control. This is the combination of sticking and following in practical application.

One other result of the sticking and following strategy is the goal of closing the distance and entering into clinch range as soon as practically possible. The longer the CIMA fighter stays in a neutral position, toe-to-toe for example, the greater the possibility he will be struck or taken down. In real fights in general, prolonged exchanges are not a good idea, and one should seek to end the fight or escape danger as quickly as possible. Whether the CIMA fighter uses the preferred strategy and initiates with an attack or the opponent attacks and he is forced to defend, the CIMA fighter will seek to maintain contact and pressure on the opponent as he seeks a superior angle, more contact and greater control. So important is the strategy of closing in on an opponent that many of the drills found in the CIMA will start from the contact position, much less time is spent initiating attacks from long range. Here again, the various push hands drills so often emphasized in the internal styles are prime examples of the heavy emphasis on close range, close contact fighting.

BAGUAZHANG TECHNIQUES

Shoulder Throw

1a The fighters are on guard. The baguazhang fighter in grey. **1b** Grey moves forward and attacks with a crashing palm strike. White defends with his right arm. The strike allows Grey to establish a connection with his opponent. **1c** Maintaining contact and constant forward sticking pressure, Grey clears White's arm with his left arm and moves in with a right elbow strike. **1d** As White deflects the elbow strike downward, Grey continues to follow White's movement and moves in with a shoulder strike to White's chest. **1e** Maintaining pressure, Grey spins counter clockwise on his right foot and swings his left leg back as he pulls White's right arm tightly over his right shoulder. Grey lowers his hips below White's hips and makes contact with his entire back. **1f** Grey shifts his weight forward and straightens his legs as he bows to throw White over his shoulder. **1g** As White lands, Grey continues to stick and follow the movement maintaining control over his downed opponent.

Follow-Up Technique: "T" Shape Shoulder Separation

2a White counters the throw by moving his hips back and pushing against Grey's lower back. **2b** Maintaining his grips, Grey follows White's motion and turns with White's defensive force. Grey turns clockwise, sticks tightly to White's shoulder with his head and threads his right arm up from below White's arm. The force bends White's arm 90°. **2c** Grey steps up with his left foot and grabs the top of his left wrist with his right hand, locking White's shoulder into his torso. **2d** Maintaining his connection to White's center through the lock, Grey simply lowers his level, causing White to fall straight onto his back. **2e** Grey continues sticking to White as he follows him to the ground. Grey drops his right knee onto White's side to control his torso as he twists White's upper arm counter clockwise to dislocate the shoulder.

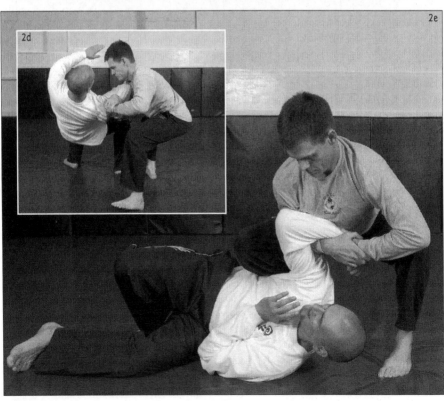

Baguazhang "Ban" Eyebrow Mopping

3a The fighters come to the on-guard position. **3b** White attacks with a right straight punch. Grey responds by slipping to his left and covering his head with his right arm as the punch goes by. **3c** Turning to his right, Grey maintains his initial contact and wraps his right arm over the top of White's right arm. At the same time, Grey strikes White in the right side of the head with a left backhand palm strike. Grey maintains contact after the strike and adheres to the side of White's head. **3d** Grey pushes White's head in a counter clockwise circle as he lowers his weight, causing White to arch over backward. **3e** Grey continues the downward spiraling pressure and brings White to the ground.

159

Follow-Up Technique: "Gua" Hip Throw

4a White counters the Eyebrow Mop by turning his head and pulling his right arm back. **4b** White continues to escape by pulling his right arm free and stepping back with his right leg. Grey follows White's motion and sticks to his right arm with his left palm. Grey simultaneously steps up with his right foot and under hooks White's left arm with his right. Note that Grey has maintained constant forward, sticking pressure with is whole body. **4c** Continuing his forward pressure, Grey steps forward with his right foot and turns his hips counter-clockwise below White's hips. Grey simultaneously pulls White's right arm down to break his posture. **4d** Grey shifts his weight forward, straightens his legs and bows to throw White over his right hip. **4e** White lands at Grey's feet.

BAGUAZHANG TECHNIQUES

"Open the Window to View the Moon" Takedown

5a The fighters square off. **5b** White begins to launch a right hook at Grey's head. Grey immediately responds by driving forward as he covers his head with his right arm in the "Tiger Hugs its Head" position. **5c** Intercepting White's force early, Grey drives his elbow into White's chest. **5d** Maintaining his sticking pressure, Grey moves in and wraps his right arm across the front of White's chest, trapping White's right arm to prevent a possible counterattack. It is important to note Grey uses his position and momentum to begin to displace White's hips toward White's right. **5e** Continuing to stick to White with his whole body, Grey turns clockwise and begins to lower his level as he grabs outside White's right knee to prevent White's escape. **5f** Grey completes the takedown by driving through White and throwing him to his rear. The throw is effected with the sticking pressure of Grey's entire body as he displaces White completely off his base.

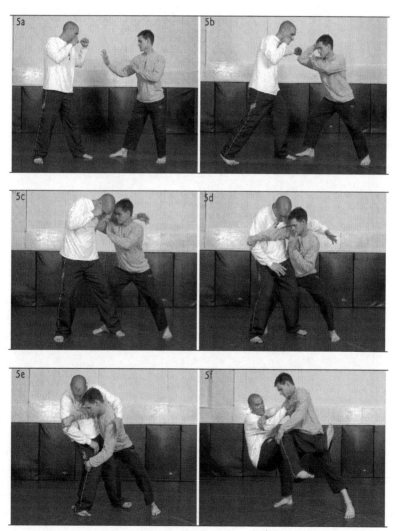

Follow-Up Technique: "Wing Blows the Lotus Leaves" Foot Sweep

6a White escapes the "Open the Window to View the Moon" takedown by shuffling away as Grey enters. **6b** Grey maintains control by following White's motion while sliding his right hand down White's right forearm to catch his wrist. **6c** Grey now pulls White's wrist to his left rear as he simultaneously sweeps White's left foot forward. **6d** White falls on his back.

Monkey Technique

7a The fighters square off. **7b** White throws a left straight punch. Grey slips the punch to the outside and simultaneously checks White's arm as he palms White in the face. Notice Grey has moved his body in as close as possible and sticks to White with his arms and chest. **7c** Maintaining contact with his left hand, Grey slides his hand around to the back of White's neck and pulls down on his head as he simultaneously knees White in the ribs. Note that Grey also has his chest adhering to White's left side. **7d** Continuing the downward pull on Grey's head, Grey lowers his left foot, turns his body counter-clockwise and leans his body weight into White. Grey immediately presses his right hip into White's left hip and slides his right leg between White's legs. As he step in, Grey wraps his right arm around the back of White's left leg. **7e** Grey continues turning counter-clockwise as he pulls down on White's head while lifting his leg. White is flipped over forward. This technique is an illustration of the sticking and following method applied when strikes and throws are used in combination. There is never a loss of contact as the internal fighter flows between percussive, grappling, and throwing techniques.

TAIJIQUAN TECHNIQUES

Zhaobao Taijiquan "Lazy About Tying Clothes" Takedown

8a The fighters are in the on guard position. **8b** Grey initiates the encounter and moves forward with a right palm strike. White defends with his right arm. **8c** Maintaining contact, Grey grabs White's right wrist and "plucks" his arm downward, passing the arm underneath his left armpit. Grey then wraps up White's right arm as he steps forward with his left foot. Notice Grey has made contact with his shoulders and chest. **8d** Grey now turns counter-clockwise and pulls White off-balance with his body weight. Grey simultaneously slides his right palm up the front of White's chest as he rotates his hips clockwise, pressing the back of his right hip into the back of White's right hip while Grey's right leg moves behind White's right leg. **8e** Grey displaces White's hips with his own as he turns counter-clockwise and lowers his weight. **8f** Grey continues the motion and pushes White's unstable body to the ground with his right hand. **8g** Grey follows White down and maintains control.

Follow-Up Technique

9a Grey steps behind White for the "lazy about tying clothes" takedown. **9b** White escapes the throw by stepping back with his right foot. Grey follows White's motion and sticks to him with his upper body. **9c** Turning counter-clockwise, Grey shuffles his left foot forward and pulls White's right arm to his left and down with his body weight as he begins to step back between White's legs with his right leg. **9d** Maintaining his upper body connection, Grey sags his weight downward and begins to sit back over his right leg. Notice Grey has wrapped White's left lower leg behind his knee. **9e** Grey sits back into White's left leg. The pressure against the inside of White's knee causes him to fall backward. **9f** The throw is completed as White lands on his back.

Zhaobao Taijiquan "Jin Gang Pounds the Pestle" Takedown

10a The fighters face off. **10b** White attacks with a right straight punch. Grey slips outside the punch and deflects the blow with the "roll back" movement. **10c** Shifting his weight forward, Grey sticks to White's arm and kicks him on the knee with his right foot. **10d** The kick causes White to move backward. Following White's motion, Grey steps his right foot down and immediately step his left foot deep behind White's base. As he steps in, Grey simultaneously lowers his weight and uses his body pressure to press White's right arm down into his side. Grey now hooks his left hand around the inside of White's left leg, preventing him from stepping back. **10e** Continuing to stick to and follow White, Grey slides his left hand down inside White's right knee and pressures forward into White. Grey displaces White's body with his own while fixing his legs in place. White flies off his base. **10f** White lands on his back.

Follow-Up Technique: "Brush Knee Angled Walk" Takedown

11a Grey is attempting the "jin gang pounds the pestle" takedown. **11b** White counters the throw by freeing his left leg and stepping away. **11c** Following White's motion, Grey adheres to the inside of White's right leg with his left arm. **11d** Turning counter-clockwise a little, Grey begins to push White's right knee back in a small clockwise circle. The angle of the pressure destabilizes White's posture. **11e** Continuing the knee push, Grey drops his right knee inward to the ground, causing him to shift his weight to his left and through White's right leg. White falls onto his back.

Conclusion

Collections of random techniques without a unifying body method and overall strategy of implementation cannot be considered martial arts. All legitimate martial arts are organized around core principles of force generation, strategy and technique. The so-called Chinese Internal Martial Arts are grouped together into a common "family" precisely because they share a common strategy of application, and by necessity related methods of generating force. From the founding query of how a smaller and weaker man may defeat a larger and stronger man in hand-to-hand combat, the concept of sticking and following was born. Once this concept was realized, it acted as the catalyst for the creation of an overall strategy of technical application, as well as necessitating a particular body method or way of generating force. It is interesting to note that any specific technique or variation thereof that can be applied according to this strategy and conforming to this body method can be adopted into the internal styles. This fact makes possible a certain degree of creativity in technical inclusion without violating the fundamental principles that make CIMA individual arts, in the true sense of the word.

Acknowledgements

I'd like to thank Jake Burroughs for posing with me in the photos. Many thanks to Dana Benjamin for her excellent photography. I'd also like to thank Brian Johnson and the North West Jiu Jitsu Academy for the use of their facility.

Sticking	Following
(zhannian)	(liansui)

index

Printed in Great Britain
by Amazon

46087234R00097